Time for Action

Stop Teaching to the Test and Start Teaching Skills

Scott D. Wurdinger

ROWMAN & LITTLEFIELD EDUCATION
A division of
ROWMAN & LITTLEFIELD PUBLISHERS, INC.
Lanham • New York • Toronto • Plymouth, UK

Published by Rowman & Littlefield Education
A division of Rowman & Littlefield Publishers, Inc.
A wholly owned subsidiary of
The Rowman & Littlefield Publishing Group, Inc.
4501 Forbes Boulevard, Suite 200, Lanham, Maryland 20706
www.rowmaneducation.com

Estover Road, Plymouth PL6 7PY, United Kingdom

British Library Cataloguing in Publication Information Available

Library of Congress Cataloging-in-Publication Data
Wurdinger, Scott D.
  Time for action : stop teaching to the test and start teaching skills /
Scott D. Wurdinger.
  p. cm.
  Includes bibliographical references.
  ISBN 978-1-61048-660-6 (cloth : alk. paper) — ISBN 978-1-61048-661-3
(pbk. : alk. paper) — ISBN 978-1-61048-662-0 (electronic)
  1. Educational tests and measurements—United States. 2. Educational
change—United States. 3. Life skills—Study and teaching—United States.
I. Title.
  LB3051.W87 2012
  371.260973—dc23

                                                                2011044789

∞TM The paper used in this publication meets the minimum requirements of
American National Standard for Information Sciences—Permanence of
Paper for Printed Library Materials, ANSI/NISO Z39.48-1992.

Printed in the United States of America

Contents

Preface

I have never felt as passionate about one of my books as I do this one. I realize readers are probably thinking that all authors say this about their own work, but this one is different for me. My previous books were for smaller audiences, mostly educators interested in implementing experiential learning in their classrooms. But this book has a much broader readership that includes everyone: parents, students, practitioners, and policy makers.

I wrote this book for anyone interested in helping to change the current education system. I wrote about my own personal experiences and the stories of others that justify the need for change. This is a practice-oriented book that contains ideas arguing why the education system must change, followed by practical ideas on how educators can implement change in their classrooms.

This book has the potential to change the way individuals view the education system, specifically the way we view the learning process. It has the potential to change the system and help create more engaging learning environments that motivate and inspire students to learn. Ultimately, it has the potential to help students become lifelong learners.

At the very core of the book is one main idea: student learning. Student learning is the most important thing that happens in education. However, in order to free up educators to use approaches that motivate students to learn, a host of other changes must occur.

Most importantly, practitioners and administrators must change their views of the learning process and see it as a process that engages students in their learning, allowing them to solve problems and learn from making mistakes. In order to motivate students to learn, they must be allowed to tap into their interests and find problems that are relevant and meaningful to them. They must be allowed to have some freedom to explore ideas and collect useful information that will help them find solutions to problems.

Learning should *not* consist of a series of standardized tests students must pass to graduate from high school and enter college. No Child Left Behind (NCLB) legislation must be eliminated or revised so that teachers can use approaches that result in experiential learning. When teachers are forced to teach to the test, they rely on the lecture method, which results in a boring learning process of rote memorization. Policy makers are the ones who can initiate changing NCLB legislation.

Education must also change its views on assessment and look for ways to assess important life skills students need to do well in school, college, and ultimately life. Without changing the current assessment system, educators will be stuck using approaches that do not motivate or inspire students to learn.

The education system is a multilayered system with the fewest number of constituents holding the most power to change policy. Students, who are the largest number of constituents, are at the opposite end of the spectrum holding the least power, but they are the ones being most negatively affected. Changing the system will require effort from all constituents, including parents and students.

I remember having a conversation with my doctoral advisor while working on my dissertation, and he gave me some advice that has stayed with me over the years. He told me to use simple words and stay clear of using jargon. He mentioned that I could use simple words but still create insightful and powerful ideas. This is what I have attempted to do in this book.

It is written with simple words that when strung together result in passionate ideas on why and how we must change the education system now. We must change it so that students can become excited and engaged in their learning and ultimately stay in school.

This is the tenth book I have authored, coauthored, or edited, and with each book I find myself evolving as a writer. My earlier books included multiple research studies and references that backed my ideas. This book provides readers with numerous stories about direct experiences of students, educators, and administrators, which include my own experiences working with students of all ages over the past twenty-six years.

The first chapter is a plea to change the current system and provides detailed information and statistics about the current state of affairs in American education. This chapter provides examples and research studies that explain why students lack interest in education today and continue to drop out at an enormous rate. If NCLB is not eliminated or revised soon, students will continue to drop out of school, increasing the pool of unskilled workers in the United States.

Chapter 2 explains why the education system should stop using high-stakes standardized tests, which results in a process of teaching to the test. It explains how the education system ended up in this situation and discusses how students have become complacent with their education.

In this chapter I offer examples of how students expect teachers to provide answers for them, which they memorize for tests. Students no longer know how to think for themselves because they are not asked to solve problems and think their way through problems to find solutions.

I explain how the problem-solving process requires a process of testing ideas against reality to determine their worth, which requires a combination of thinking and doing. Students are not asked to think critically; instead they are asked to memorize more and more information for tests. Raising standards today means increasing the amount of information that should be memorized for tests.

Finally, I offer examples of certain schools that have changed their views of learning and how these schools focus their teaching on life skills as much as they do on their academic skills. Research shows how these schools are graduating students who have learned important life skills that helped them navigate their way through college and are providing them with the confidence to become self-directed learners.

Chapter 3 provides practitioners with ideas on how to use teaching approaches that increase engagement and allow students to learn life skills such as problem solving, time management, and responsibility. Examples of extracurricular activities are provided that explain why students gravitate toward these activities. Students are allowed to be involved in extracurricular activities on a deeper level and learn skills through their participation. They are allowed to practice different types of skills and are able to see themselves improve over time.

The next section of this chapter provides information on how to implement five different teaching approaches that include challenge-based learning, project-based learning, collaborative learning, problem-based learning, and service learning. The information in this section was written primarily for practitioners and explains useful information that will allow educators to implement these concepts in their own classrooms.

The last section of this chapter explains why teaching skills helps promote rigor and relevance in the learning process. When educators focus on teaching skills, students become excited about learning and are able to see themselves improve in their skill level over time. Motivation to learn is no longer a concern for educators using approaches that focus on skill development.

Chapter 4 takes an in-depth look at current standards and benchmarks and argues for a different set of standards that focus on developing life skills. Most states' current standards and benchmarks are numerous, and educators are pinched for time to cover them all.

This results in a situation where teachers must quickly cover all the material by the end of the term so that students can be tested on this information. Educators do not have enough time to adequately cover all the material and provide students with opportunities to apply what they are learning. Educators end up teaching to the test, and students end up being bored with this process.

Adopting the National Core Standards could help alleviate this problem. The National Standards have fewer standards, so educators would be able to cover them more adequately and could do it in a way that allows students to practice life skills. The system needs to eliminate or at least minimize the number of state standards and benchmarks and adopt the National Standards, which will allow educators to go deeper into the content and worry less about breadth.

Finally, this chapter discusses the importance of having students create products and conduct presentations. Creating products and presentations will allow students to design and build things, which helps them develop life skills.

When students are responsible for creating projects and products, they must learn how to manage their time, be responsible to group members for completing their tasks, and test out their ideas to find solutions. They will learn how to organize and present their ideas to peers and educators, learning valuable life skills that they can carry with them throughout life.

Chapter 5 discusses how we should prepare teacher candidates to teach in new schools that are using experiential approaches to learning. New schools are cropping up all over the country that use innovative approaches to teaching and learning. Teacher candidates must be educated about these new school models and learn how to use these new approaches to learning.

The next section of this chapter identifies six organizations that are developing new schools and programs using new approaches that focus on student learning. In addition, six key stakeholders from these organizations were interviewed and asked what teacher education programs should be doing differently to train candidates to teach in their schools.

They were also asked what their organizations do to train educators to teach in their schools. Their responses to these questions suggest that current teacher education programs are not educating candidates to teach in their schools, and so they are providing their own training programs for their practitioners.

Chapter 6 consists of final thoughts on key issues that must change in order for the education system to move forward in a positive direction and provide students with opportunities to become more engaged in their learning. Views on learning, NCLB legislation, and assessment systems must change so that students can become motivated to learn life skills that they need to become productive members of society.

There are many people I would like to thank for helping me pull the information together for this book. As always my family, Annette, Madeline, and Lauren, allowed me to take time away from them and spend numerous hours alone with my laptop computer writing down my thoughts.

I would like to thank Tom Koerner and the individuals from Rowman and Littlefield for reading, editing, and producing this book. Tom was especially helpful in offering edits.

Two of my longtime colleagues, Jeff Boeke and David Lockett, listened to my stories about the negative and positive impacts of the education system on students and offered their ideas about what to include in the book that would help improve the system.

My core group of friends, who are business owners and administrators, allowed me to discuss my ideas about how students lack life skills and provided me with examples of their own personal experiences hiring young workers lacking these types of skills. These people included Dick and Terry Kakeldey, Randy and Jean Farrow, Mark and Jane Lange, Bob and Pam Jagdfeld, and Ernie and Liliya Comeaux.

Thanks to Doug Thomas, Scott Hartl, Elliot Washor, Ben Daley, Tim Presiado, and Stephen Rice for giving me their time to interview them. Their insights and ideas on teacher preparation programs and training teachers for their schools were invaluable.

Jim Wartman and Jose Garcia provided me with a wealth of information on how to implement project-based learning and challenge-based learning in the classroom. They are seasoned educators who understand better than most how to use these approaches.

Thanks to my colleague Jerry Robicheau for doing a thorough reading of the book and providing superb feedback that helped me form my thoughts in the early stages of writing the book.

Julie Carlson, my department chair, gave me some wonderful ideas during our discussions on various topics contained in the book.

Thanks to Doug Thomas, Bob Wedl, Tony Wagner, and Stephen Brookfield for taking the time to read the book and write their endorsements. I would also like to thank Jen Rudolph for providing feedback, especially on the book's title.

Finally, I would like to thank my research partner Walter Enloe for providing information on how to incorporate our research studies into the book. His thoughts and ideas are always an inspiration to me!

Chapter One

Time for Action

I watched a dramatic deterioration in my daughter's happiness when she entered high school. Not long ago she came up from the basement, sat down in between my wife and me, and started crying. I immediately started asking her questions. Did you break up with your boyfriend? Are you having problems with your friends? Are you having problems at school? Are you sad because you don't like yourself? The questions continued with no answers. Finally she confided that she was depressed and anxious about her life and felt too much pressure to do well in school.

There has been a slow evolution where anxiety and despair has crept into my daughter. She was always bubbly and energetic as a child and loved going to her elementary school. She would come home from school and talk about how much she liked her teachers and told us every detail about her school day and the activities that captured her interest.

Middle school was very similar, with teachers who were funny and engaging, and projects in which she immersed herself. Projects were common in middle school, and she loved learning because her teachers knew how to engage students in their learning.

Then came high school, and along with it a complete transformation of her personality. She was no longer bubbly and energetic about school and would often ask if we could call the school to excuse her from going on certain days. She no longer has a sparkle in her eye when it comes to learning and rarely tells us anything about school. She is quiet and somber and seems sad much of the time. We have to persistently prod her with questions in order to find out what is going on in her classes. Learning is no longer fun and exciting for her.

She came home from school one day and said to me, "Dad, I don't even know why we have teachers." I asked her to explain and she responded by saying, "I know how to read the books, figure out what is going to be on the tests, and take the tests." If this is what education has evolved into, then she might be correct.

My daughter has always been an excellent student, but I believe she has reached a saturation point. She does not like school anymore, and for the first time in her high school experience her grades have dropped significantly. She knows how to take tests and has always been a straight-A student, but she no longer sees the point. School is no longer relevant to her.

Her experience is not uncommon. In the video *Race to Nowhere*, directed by Vickie Abeles, students talk about the stresses of school and the enormous pressure placed on them to succeed and get into a good college. Several students mention that school has created anxiety and depression for them.

Academic success is all about high test scores. Students go from one class to the next and listen to teachers tell them what they need to learn for the test. This does not create an exciting learning environment. Today's students are passive learners and are not allowed to be engaged in the learning process. They are not allowed to explore their own interests and learn about things that are relevant and important to them. They are forced to learn the content benchmarks and are tested on them.

In the High School Survey of Student Engagement, a vast majority of students said they were bored every day in school, with reasons that included uninteresting material that was not relevant and a lack of interaction with teachers (Yazzie-Mintz, 2006). If policy makers, administrators, and educators do not change their own views on learning and what it means to be an educated citizen, large numbers of high school and college students will continue to drop out each year, primarily because they are frustrated and bored with the education they are receiving (Bridgeland, DiIulio, & Morison, 2006; Wolk, 2001). Educators must change the way they conduct business in their learning environments by changing their teaching practices, but in order to do this, policy makers must change legislation and create new laws that move away from high-stakes standardized tests as the way to measure academic success.

The education system tends to view academic achievement as the ability to memorize information for tests. Schools that are identified as successful are those that meet Adequate Yearly Progress (AYP) requirements and have a high acceptance rate into college, both of which require high test scores. However, many students find memorizing information for these tests tedious and boring, requiring hours of reciting information over and over in their heads until it sticks. Many students are not skilled at memorizing information nor do they enjoy it, yet it continues to be the dominant learning process promoted by schools and colleges.

The overemphasis on testing has led to a situation where some parents in Pennsylvania are opting to pull their children out of the state-mandated tests (Levitt & Candiotti, 2011). A handful of parents went to their children's school in State College, Pennsylvania, and told the administrators that their children were not going to take the required state-mandated tests. These parents are frustrated and believe that these tests must be eliminated from education because they do not measure a student's ability to succeed, and they should not be used to evaluate a school's performance. Maybe this act could lead to a nationwide movement!

Howard Gardner, professor of cognition and education at the Harvard Graduate School of Education, suggests that there are eight intelligences, which include linguistics, logical-mathematical, spatial, bodily-kinesthetic, musical, interpersonal, intrapersonal, and naturalist (2006, pp. 8–18), and he believes that people have a dominant intelligence that they rely on when learning information. Education however seems to neglect individual learning styles and instead forces all students to use the same learning process, which is memorization of information.

Standardized education moves students from the same grade level, through the same curriculum, at the same pace, taking the same tests, at the same time. In order to move away from memorization as the dominant learning process toward one that inspires and motivates students to learn, education must change its views on learning and teaching.

This book is not about large-scale reforms or changing the entire American education system. Books have been written about why significant large-scale reforms are necessary in order to improve the American education system, but my book will focus primarily on one aspect of education: changing our teaching approaches so that students become excited about learning again. However, in order to change our teaching approaches, assessment procedures must change as well, which will free up educators to use approaches that motivate students to learn.

After teaching in higher education for twenty-one years, it is my firm belief that when students are engaged in direct experiences they become inspired and motivated to learn more. Activities, projects, and experiences outside the classroom allow them to become engaged in their learning while practicing important life skills that go above and beyond academic learning. My past conversations with parents affirm my belief because when I ask them, "What do you want your child to learn from his or her education?" the answers focus primarily on the development of life skills such as responsibility, integrity, honesty, and self-directed learning.

Peter Temes published a book titled *Against School Reform and in Praise of Great Teaching* (2003) and argues that there have been multiple attempts over the years to reform American education that have failed, so instead of creating more reforms we should focus on effective teaching practices that give teachers the freedom to experiment with different approaches. While this is an excellent idea, it won't work until we eliminate the current assessment system that prevents educators from using teaching approaches that engage students in their learning.

The U.S. government must pass new legislation that eliminates high-stakes standardized multiple-choice tests so that educators are free to use different approaches. The current assessment system is forcing educators to teach to the test, and the result of this process is students who do not know how to think or solve problems. Students should be demonstrating knowledge and practicing life skills rather than memorizing information.

I have spent many hours as an educator listening to people talk about their ideas on how to change things to improve education. I have watched numerous news programs in which experts discuss how we need to make policy changes in our country to improve education. I have listened to politicians talk about their ideas on how to raise test scores, and if elected, how they will make these changes a reality. At the university where I work I listen to professors talk about how we need to change things in education. But all of these discussions focus on one result—raising test scores. Higher test scores is not the answer—different test scores is!

New types of tests, which allow students to demonstrate knowledge and practice skills, will allow teachers to use innovative approaches that inspire and motivate students to learn meaningful skills. Frankly, I am tired of listening to all the discussions on how to raise test scores. It is time to take action and stop all the talking. We need to change things now. NO MORE TALKING, IT'S TIME FOR ACTION!

Diane Ravitch (2010) and Tony Wagner (2008) have written comprehensive books on the state of education in America, identifying the pitfalls with NCLB and its extreme emphasis on testing. These are insightful books that explain why we are in need of a renaissance in American education and the importance of changing our current educational systems. I worry, however, that once again policy makers, administrators, and educators will read these books and agree that they are right on the mark, but they will not result in any meaningful change that needs to occur right now.

According to Arne Duncan (2010, p. 3), the secretary of education, we are losing 1.2 million students each year, perhaps because many of them are bored with their education. Both high school and college students are dropping out because educators continue to focus on the wrong results in education—standardized test scores. Educators need to provide students with meaningful learning that inspires them to learn, rather than providing them with more Scantron tests that do not mean anything to them.

In 1991 Howard Gardner stated that, "In the course of their careers in the American schools of today, most students take hundreds, if not thousands, of tests. They develop skill to a highly calibrated degree in an exercise that will essentially become useless immediately after their last day in school" (1991, p. 216). Sadly enough, twenty years later, the education system is still using standardized tests as the measuring stick for intelligence in the United States.

Some people I talk to think that I am too radical with my ideas and tell me that I should not be writing a book like this one. But I don't think I am too radical. I teach my classes, attend meetings, and follow many of the rules and policies at my university. I am not a nonconformist.

I do know, however, that the current education system is not working. Students are frustrated, bored, and disengaged from learning, yet the system continues to raise standards, which means raising test scores.

I have taught hundreds of high-school-age students in nontraditional learning environments, and I do know from these experiences that students excel when they are involved in relevant hands-on activities. I was a biology major and taught science classes at nature centers and environmental learning centers, and I also taught science courses to high school Upward Bound students.

During these experiences it became obvious that students love to learn when they are immersed in direct experience and are learning skills. When you give students something to do that requires them to solve a problem, they will engage themselves in learning without even realizing they are learning. If anything, my background is just right for writing about the need for action and integrating experiential learning in the classroom.

My life has been filled with naysayers who told me I should not go to college because I was not smart enough, should not get a master's degree because I could not write well enough, should not get a PhD because I would never finish writing a dissertation, would not get tenured because I could not do the right type of research, and now, cannot write this book because it is too radical. Why are there so many naysayers in education, people who want to block you from learning and bettering yourself?

On the opposite side, I have had a handful of friends who are encouraging me to write this book. They get just as fired up as I am when I tell them that I am writing to policy makers, administrators, teachers, and students to take action and stop using tests that force students to memorize bits and pieces of information disconnected from their lives. These friends are not in the field of education; they are lawyers, financial planners, directors of psychiatric facilities, and a host of other business professionals.

Ironically, the ones who are supporting me are mostly Republicans who have liberal views on education and conservative views on politics. This is the reverse of many of the doubters who are mostly Democrats who have liberal views on politics but conservative views on education. This has been a confusing paradox for me. One would assume that academics in higher education, who are mostly Democrats, would be open to new ideas, promoting academic freedom, and experimenting with new techniques and approaches. But they are not. They want to maintain the status quo.

The doubters do not want to change. They continue to teach the same way and hold fast to tradition. They assume that low test scores mean that you are not smart enough to attend college, but maybe students are bored with these tests and don't care anymore about how well they do on them. Maybe some of these students are actually smart but just don't care anymore.

My personal experience with education was filled with lectures and tests. I was bored most of the time and as a result received average grades that almost kept me from attending college. I can relate to how many college students are feeling today because it took me eight years to complete my undergraduate degree, not because I was a bad student, but because I wanted to experience the things I was reading about in my classes. I needed to make sense of the material I was reading, so I took time off from college to experience some of the things I was reading about in my textbooks.

Theory, compartmentalized bits and pieces of information, and bubble tests did not cut it for me. I needed to get out of the classroom and experience things firsthand. So, I feel that I am not a radical, but rather a realist who believes in using learning approaches that connect with students, approaches that motivate and inspire them to learn.

I was lucky to even attend college. My parents wanted me to attend but told me they did not have the money to pay for any of my college expenses. Furthermore, my high school guidance counselor told me I would never make it through college and suggested that I attend a trade school where I could learn a skill. The reason I made it through a bachelor's degree, two master's degrees, and a PhD is that I focused most of my efforts on applying my book learning and translating it into direct experience.

I have navigated my way through the education system as a student and as a professor, and I realize that there are many students not as fortunate as I have been who drop out of education because they are told they are not smart enough or because they are just plain bored with their education. High school and college students continue to drop out at an astronomical rate, so educators need to change their teaching approaches soon, or we will continue to lose students who are bright but bored. The unemployment rate will continue to grow with unskilled young dropouts. Here are several revealing facts about attrition rates and causes of attrition rates for high school and college students:

- Approximately 30 percent of high school students who start high school drop out (Greene & Winters, 2006).
- Eighty-eight percent of high school dropouts have passing grades (Bridgeland, DiIulio, & Morison, 2006).
- Fifty percent of high school dropouts leave because they are bored (Bridgeland, DiIulio, & Morison, 2006).
- "Boring" was the number-one word chosen by high schoolers that best described their high school experience (Wolk, 2001).

- "Nothing" was the number-one choice by high schoolers when asked what they liked best about school (Wolk, 2001).
- The national five-year rate of college baccalaureate completion is less than 50 percent (Astin & Oseguera, 2002).
- One primary reason for dropping out of college is poor or indifferent teaching (Levitz, Noel, & Richter, 1999).

Numerous high school and college students are dropping out every year because they are not finding any meaningful purpose in their education. This has to change now. Who has the power to make these changes happen? Is it policy makers, administrators, or educators?

What I am about to propose in this book may cause some uneasy feelings among these individuals. Policy makers should eliminate assessment systems that use standardized tests, and administrators should stop supporting the use of these tests and refuse to have teachers give them to their students. By eliminating these tests, teachers would no longer feel pressured to teach to the test. Teachers would no longer have to rely on the lecture method to quickly spoon out information in order to cover the hundreds of standards and benchmarks. Teachers could take back their classrooms and teach using more creative methods that engage students in their learning, rather than continuing to teach to the test.

A governmental policy is mandating and dictating most of what teachers do in their classrooms, and raising test scores is not a fair approach in holding teachers accountable. The current assessment system needs to be replaced with one that will promote more meaningful learning in the classroom, one that can give teachers some freedom to determine their own teaching approaches.

A sobering report published by the Center on Education Policy (2010) recently came out on the efficacy of No Child Left Behind. The bottom line is, it does not work! In Minnesota, where I live, over half the schools in the state did not make AYP. Here are some other key findings of this report:

- About one-third of U.S. public schools did not make AYP based on tests administered in school year 2008–2009.
- In nine states and the District of Columbia, at least half the public schools did not make AYP in 2008–2009.

• In a majority of the states (thirty-four including D.C.), at least one-fourth of the schools did not make AYP.

The percentage of public schools not making AYP varied greatly by state, from 5 percent in Texas to 77 percent in Florida. These differences among states do not necessarily reflect the quality of schools; rather, they are likely due to state variations in standards, tests, cut scores for proficient performance on those tests, and methods for calculating AYP (Center on Education Policy, 2010, p. 2).

States have figured out that if they don't make AYP, they can lower the standards for the tests, making the questions easier. In essence, schools are dumbing down the tests in order to improve their chances of making AYP. There is an interesting irony here; just like students who are constantly trying to figure out how to beat the system and get a better grade, so too are educators trying to figure out how to beat the system and raise their class test scores. What is the point of these tests if the education system continues to lower the standards? Why does the education system continue to use these types of tests?

The report also mentioned that if AYP is not replaced there is a strong chance that in some states nearly all schools could be labeled as failing by the school year 2013. The report concludes that AYP must be eliminated and replaced with a different type of evaluation system.

Educators talk about raising the standards, but what does that mean? Does it mean making the tests harder? Does it mean including more questions on the tests? Raising standards usually implies raising test scores, but these are not the only standards that matter, and they certainly do not effectively measure a person's ability to succeed in life. Maybe the standards should focus more on the student's ability to apply information. Maybe they should concentrate on measuring life skills that are essential for succeeding in the workplace, and in life in general.

We need to look for other ways to assess students. Rather than using multiple-choice tests, we should be using performance as an assessment technique. Multiple-choice tests focus on memorization, whereas performance assessments are based on application of information. If teachers want to find out how much their students know, they should ask students what they know or have students show them. Have students tell educators what they know. When students do presentations, they have to explain what they know. This type of assessment shows teachers exactly what students know.

When using standardized multiple-choice tests, students can use a process of elimination and make educated guesses allowing for the possibility of a high score. With presentations there is no guessing. Students must explain what they know, which allows the educator to more accurately assess their knowledge.

Two questions educators need to ask themselves are, what should be assessed, and how should it be assessed? Currently, K–12 public education, and in many cases colleges and universities, assesses only academic skills, but educators should also be assessing life skills such as problem solving, creativity, teamwork, and self-directed learning.

Life skills are extremely important because they are the ones students most need when they leave school and enter the work world. Life skills are the ones that employers are looking for in their employees. Educators can assess both academic and life skills through demonstration and performance, which will challenge students intellectually and provide more meaningful learning for both educators and students.

Performance assessments are more challenging because students have to take their learning to the next level, which is explaining or showing what they know. The process is not just cerebral; students must demonstrate what they know, which requires direct involvement from the student. This process teaches students important public speaking skills and forces them to synthesize the material and make sense out of it for themselves.

This process also teaches students important critical thinking skills because they have to formalize their thoughts and organize them into a coherent speech. Students want to be challenged; they are bored when they have to sit and listen to teachers all day. When educators make learning active, students become more involved and will often rise to the challenge. Life skills such as creativity and problem solving are the types of skills educators should be assessing. These are the skills that will allow students to do well in life after they graduate.

Policy makers need to change the current assessment system and create a new one. Administrators and educators need to put a stop to high-stakes standardized tests and give students opportunities to explore new learning and to demonstrate what they know. Educators need to get students excited about learning and provide them freedom to explore some of their own interests in education. If schools don't stop using standardized tests now, the system will continue to lose students.

Educators have attempted to make learning objective by creating tests with right and wrong answers, but what does this really measure? It measures how well students can memorize information. But real learning is not strictly objective. It is a messy process, which includes creating plans and testing them against reality. It includes multiple trial-and-error attempts that allow students to learn from making mistakes.

This process is what learning is all about, and it is what life is all about. The education system has created a complex assessment process, which does not have to be complicated. In the business world, individuals are evaluated by their performance, and employers have discussions with employees to find out what they know and what their ideas are to improve the company and business. Ask students to demonstrate their knowledge and explain it. It's that simple.

Educators need to minimize standardized tests, teaching to the test, lecturing, and using memorization as the primary learning process. None of these things result in meaningful learning for students. These things result in boredom and push students away from school. New assessment tools need to be created that evaluate student performance and allow students to demonstrate their learning through active participation in their education.

The time has come for action! The deeper question is, will policy makers have the courage to take action and make some changes in the current public education and higher education systems so there are fewer tests and more direct experiences in our classroom learning environments? Will policy makers create a different assessment system that allows educators to develop exciting learning environments where students are inspired and motivated to learn, or will they continue to follow the status quo?

I do not have the same pedigree as some of the folks that I reference in this book, and I did not graduate from an Ivy League school. Therefore this book might not sit on the same shelf as Ravitch's, Wagner's, or Gardner's, but no one will convince me that the ideas in this book are of any less importance than the ideas contained in their books.

I would like to throw out a challenge to the publisher of this book, and they can certainly take it out of any royalties I might garner from them. I would like to have this book sent to every commissioner of education in all fifty states. This is at least one attempt to take action now. Commissioners, take a stance and say no to NCLB high-stakes tests.

Chapter Two

Stop High-Stakes Standardized Testing and Teaching to the Test

How did the education system end up in this situation? In 2001 No Child Left Behind (NCLB) was passed and states began creating curriculum standards. After the standards were developed, standardized tests were created to assess students' knowledge of these standards. When student test scores became the mechanism to assess student learning, as well as to hold teachers accountable, teachers began teaching to the test. The most efficient way to teach to the test is by using the lecture format because it allows teachers to dole out large amounts of information in short amounts of time. The problem, however, is that this method kills motivation and inspiration to learn.

Curriculum standards are obviously important in piquing student interest, but even the best curriculum standards in the world will not sink into the heads of students if they are poorly delivered. In her book *The Death and Life of the Great American School System* (2010), Diane Ravitch talks about the importance of first developing a strong curriculum, but a strong curriculum delivered poorly for the purpose of raising test scores will leave our students bored and disengaged.

Most educators can agree on the ends of education. Leaving no child behind is an admirable goal, but what means should educators use to get there? The means used to get to the end are just as important as, if not more important than, the end itself; and as long as NCLB is in place teachers will continue to teach to the test as a means to deliver information to students.

I have served on several curriculum committees and have spent a fair number of hours mapping curriculum standards and content. This was a useful endeavor; however, we should have spent an equal amount of time discussing delivery methods. If a teacher relies solely on direct instruction, then the most important content may be nothing more than a meaningless string of words coming out of the teacher's mouth. If students are forced to be passive learners and sit and listen to teachers talk all day, then it doesn't matter what is said in the lecture; deep learning and the ability to apply information will not happen.

In a book that I coauthored with my colleague Julie Carlson titled *Teaching for Experiential Learning* (2009), we discuss multiple studies that explain the disadvantages of using the lecture method. These studies make it obvious that this method does not inspire students to learn (Blackburn, Pellino, Boberg, & O'Connell, 1980; Huba & Freed, 2000; Sax, Keup, Gilmartin, Stolzenberg, & Harper, 2002). When I walk through the halls of my building I observe firsthand the negative effects of lecturing—students nodding off, texting on their phones, and working on their laptops completely disengaged from the lecture.

The most relevant research that explains why students are not listening suggests that it is because their attention span is only fifteen to twenty minutes (Hoover, 2006; Middendorf & Kalish, 1996). They lose interest in a lecture if it goes beyond this time limit. Other studies in our book explain that students are just bored with the education they are receiving, primarily because they are not allowed to participate and be actively engaged in the learning process.

Think about this for a moment: What are the most important skills students should learn today while in high school and college? Do you agree that life skills such as problem solving, creativity, collaboration, and self-directed learning are some of the most important skills a student should learn? If so, then why do policy makers, administrators, and educators continue to support multiple-choice standardized tests as the best way to measure intelligence?

What skills are students learning when they take these tests? Are they learning how to solve problems, be creative, and become self-directed learners? Oddly enough, people believe in the value of life skills yet continue to use a process that results in a mind-numbing process that leads to apathy and boredom!

Are the current education systems in the United States, both in higher education and public high school education, based on a false assumption? What if intelligence was based on one's ability to apply information rather than one's ability to memorize it? What if the best way to measure a person's intelligence was not through standardized testing but through performance testing?

Currently, intelligence, and one's ability to succeed, is based on how well students perform on standardized multiple-choice tests, but one's ability to apply information is a better learning process, so unfortunately most of what educators, schools, and educational systems are currently promoting is an inadequate learning process.

Textbooks are written to cover the state's curriculum standards, teachers lecture and teach to the test, students memorize the information and take the tests, and all of this centers on one goal: raising test scores. However, these types of tests do not promote a meaningful learning process that motivates students. The data that are used to drive instructional practices in order to meet AYP focus on the wrong goal.

When the goal is high test scores, students are forced to memorize information, which does not allow them to become creative thinkers and self-directed learners. Students are forced to remember facts that have little meaning in their lives. The government continues to hold schools and colleges accountable for test scores, but these are the wrong types of tests. Educators should be using assessment tools that measure important skills such as problem solving, creativity, and self-directed learning.

If the primary underlying assumption is wrong, then everything that emanates from that assumption is also wrong. A huge bureaucracy based on high-stakes tests has been created, which is based on an incorrect assumption, and it all comes back to the teachers and students. Teachers and students are the pawns in the system and are being held accountable for an inadequate process of learning.

Teachers need to be treated as professionals. Currently, most everything teachers do in their classrooms is based on NCLB. They are trapped, and this legislation is not only stifling the creativity in students but it is stifling teacher creativity as well. Teachers are the professionals and should be managing their own classrooms according to what they believe is in the best interests of their students.

The number-one most important thing that occurs in schools, colleges, and universities is what happens in the classroom between educators and students. Everything else is secondary. Educators should be challenging students to think, providing them with opportunities to be creative, letting them work in groups so they learn how to collaborate, and letting them learn by making mistakes. NCLB testing policies and procedures have created a death grip on teachers that prevents them from exercising their own judgment on how to best educate their students.

Teachers are obsessed with increasing test scores because their livelihoods depend on it. There are cases where not only are students cheating, but teachers are cheating as well on several different levels (Amrein-Beardsley, Berliner, & Rideau, 2010). Teachers are resorting to cheating because their jobs are at stake.

Public education and higher education are producing students who simply cannot think for themselves. Students have learned how to retain large amounts of information and how to do well on tests, but they don't know how to solve problems. When placed in situations where they are forced to solve a problem, many are paralyzed. Students are not learning how to be self-directed because the system always provides the answers for them. How can students become self-directed learners if they are never given opportunities in school to make mistakes and figure things out on their own?

In K–12 education, NCLB legislation has created this problem, and teachers are stuck in a system that is measuring the wrong thing. Everything that has been created in the U.S. education system, such as standards-based curriculums, data-driven instruction, high-stakes standardized tests, and Adequate Yearly Progress reports, are all measuring the wrong outcome.

Undergraduate education is somewhat similar. The same learning process carries over from high school to college. College classes are often fifty minutes in length, which makes it challenging for educators to engage students in any meaningful discussion or hands-on learning. The lecture is the most common teaching method, which is typically followed by quizzes and exams. Education at both levels has it all wrong!

Learning is about using a complex process that involves multiple steps and multiple trial-and-error episodes where students make mistakes and learn how to improve upon their solutions through these mistakes. According to John Dewey, who wrote volumes of information on using direct experience for learning, the problem-solving process entails identifying a problem, making a plan to solve it, testing the plan to see if it works, and reflecting on how to improve upon the solution (as cited in McDermott, 1973, pp. 101–119).

This process engages students in their learning because students are thinking, planning, and testing ideas, as opposed to just remembering facts. Thinking is a more complex process than remembering information, and it is an essential skill to survive in today's world. Life outside of school requires us to solve problems every day, yet students lack this skill because they are too busy reciting information in their heads for tests.

The skills students are learning are not the skills they need to succeed in life. Measuring life skills such as problem solving and creativity may be challenging. However, if the education system does not start teaching these skills, the problem will persist, resulting in more inept problem solvers in the United States.

Through his research Tony Wagner identified a list of skills that employers believe are essential for students to have once they enter the work world. These skills are problem solving, collaboration, agility, initiative, oral and written communication, assessing information, and curiosity (2008, pp. 14–38). Employers are interested in hiring individuals who have the ability to ask probing questions, can solve critical problems, can be productive team players, and are able to adapt to ever-changing work environments.

The skills Wagner identifies are similar to the skills identified in the Secretary's Commission on Achieving Necessary Skills (SCANS) report titled *What Work Requires of Schools*, published in 2000. This report found that skills such as creative thinking, decision making, problem solving, knowing how to learn, and reasoning were the skills employers valued the most but were lacking in their young new hires.

The Partnership for 21st Century Skills is another organization that is promoting the development of life skills students need to be successful once they leave school and enter the work world. These skills are similar to the ones Wagner and the SCANS report identified. Some of the skills they are promoting include critical thinking and problem solving, communication, collaboration, and creativity and innovation (Partnership for 21st Century Skills website, n.d.). This organization has developed resources and tools that educators can use to help students develop these skills.

Employers want to hire individuals who are curious about how the organization operates and are able to speak and write effectively. The bottom line is they want people who are self-directed and can figure things out on their own. These skills are essential to survival in today's world, but Wagner found that they are sorely lacking in high school and college graduates.

Andrea Batista Schlesinger argues the same point as Wagner. In her book, appropriately titled *The Death of Why*, she states, "America's employers aren't interested in test scores; they are interested in people who can think, question, adapt, and perform. We have created an educational environment devoid of curiosity, creativity and inquiry" (2009, p. 6). She believes the education system is handing out answers to questions so that students can do well on tests, and this process is causing our students to no longer question anything. If they need answers they simply turn to the computer and find them on Google or other search engines.

My experience teaching undergraduate students, as well as working with public schools, affirms Wagner's and Schlesinger's research. Two examples are particularly poignant. The first occurred when I was teaching a freshman undergraduate course in theories and practices of experiential learning and started a discussion on different learning theories. I began asking questions about how students like to learn best, and as students answered my questions, I continued to probe with more questions. After several minutes of discussion one student interrupted me and asked, "Why are you doing this to us?" I was taken aback and asked, "Why am I doing what?" His response was, "Making us think." He continued by saying, "Why don't you just give us the answers you want so we can learn them for the test?"

The second example occurred when I was working with a local school district and realized that their schools were not providing students with problem-solving skills, so they made it a district goal. I was surprised when I read this goal in their list of district goals, and I told the principal of the school that problem solving should be woven into all classes and subjects at the school. He hired me to come in and teach problem solving as a separate goal detached from any subjects, but I told him that it would have to be connected to all subjects. I found it hard to believe that they actually identified problem solving as a district goal, which proved to me that educators and administrators in this district realized their students were lacking in problem-solving skills because they were spending the majority of their time focusing on test-taking skills.

Students have been inculcated with a process of getting the answers they need and remembering them long enough to take the test. This problem is not going away, and it is not the students' fault. The longer our government continues to promote this type of learning, the more severe this problem will become. Educators need to change their focus from answers to questions, from content to process. Educators need to use a different learning process that will help students become problem solvers before they enter the work world.

My daughter recently applied for a college loan and had to participate in an online loan counseling session in order to get the loan. The online session required students to read about eight pages of information and then take a quiz at the end of the reading material. As I watched her I realized she had quickly clicked to the end of the reading material and was focusing her attention on the quiz questions. Within about five minutes she finished the quiz and scored 100 percent, without ever reading any of the content.

I was amazed and asked her how she did it. She told me that she found all the answers by Googling the questions. She knew how to find the answers without ever reading a single word of the content. Students know how to find answers, but what are they comprehending when they engage in this process?

Students have learned how to use technology to find answers, and they know how to quickly peruse textbooks to find answers they need for their worksheet assignments. They have become very skilled at using technology for finding answers, which makes sense, because most schools and colleges focus their learning outcomes on knowing the correct answers. Students have learned how to be efficient at finding answers and have become adept at this skill, but what type of learning process is occurring in their brains? My daughter can find the answers, but what about her ability to solve more complex problems, especially those that will crop up in the workplace when she enters that arena?

Students have become complacent and expect teachers and employers to give them the answers. They search, find, and plug in the answers. Their brains are not being used to create a plan and test it out to determine if the plan worked. They have become entirely cerebral and lack the ability to solve real-life problems. Challenging real-world problems need to be provided in all subject areas so that students can practice and learn how to think for themselves.

At the high school level, NCLB is the culprit of this problem, and until it is replaced by other legislation, nothing will change. Teachers will continue to dole out information that students need to remember for tests, and lecturing will be the primary teaching method used for this purpose.

Similar assessments have been created in higher education, and the problem is no different at this level. Assessment meetings are fairly common at universities and are used to teach faculty how to input student scores into these assessment software programs. Test scores are one of the predominant pieces of data entered into these software assessment programs, which implies that the same problem exists in higher education.

Using software programs to input test data has its own unique problem. The focus of many collegewide assessment meetings I have attended is on how to input data into the software program. Faculty concentrate their efforts on learning how to use the software program, so the real focus, which should be improving student learning, is lost when faculty are immersed in trying to figure out how to input the data. It is easy to lose focus and become more concerned with how to input data as opposed to how to improve student learning.

Schools are beginning to implement reforms to help teachers improve their teaching, but in a similar vein the focus is often misdirected to the procedures instead of the real goal of helping students learn. For example, during one of my university classes, middle school and high school teachers began discussing the pros and cons of their professional learning communities (PLC).

The purpose of a PLC is for teachers to spend time together discussing what is working and what is not working in their classrooms, and to share ideas on how to improve student learning. One of the teachers was furious with the PLC process because he said they spent most of their time during the meeting documenting how they were being accountable for their meeting time. They had little or no time to discuss problems and concerns in their classrooms. He said the PLC did not help his group improve anything.

Accountability is a huge issue in education today. Administrators are holding teachers accountable for not only their students' test scores, but also for professional development opportunities such as PLCs. But what does it mean to be accountable? Should accountability be based on paper documents that show improved test scores and what teachers did with their PLC time?

How should teachers be held accountable? If we agree that learning life skills should be a primary learning outcome, then it appears that accountability is also based on a false assumption. Maybe teachers should be held accountable for inspiring students to become lifelong learners, teaching them how to solve problems, and teaching them how to be more creative.

In Newell and Van Ryzin's book *Assessing What Really Matters in Schools* (2009), they argue that schools are assessing the wrong thing. They argue that teachers should not be using test scores to assess how much information students can memorize, but rather education should be assessing the students' level of hope for the future and motivation to learn. When students increase hope and motivation, they learn because they want to learn and are optimistic about their future.

The education system needs to be looking at assessing other types of skills that students need to succeed in life. Memorization is a skill that is basically useless once students graduate from college. The United States is now a culture of technology, and information is easily accessible through computers. There is no need to memorize mountains of information in high school or college because students can quickly access it when they need it.

Today's students are racing ahead of their educators and learning in spite of the education they are receiving in formal schooling. They are using technology that in many cases their teachers are unaware of or unfamiliar with. Clayton Christensen, Curtis Johnson, and Michael Horn wrote a book titled *Disrupting Class: How Disruptive Innovation Will Change the Way the World Learns*, which suggests that the monolithic approach to education, consisting of the teacher providing students with information that they memorize for tests, will soon become a thing of the past. Technology is disrupting education, and teachers will have to learn how to use digital technology in order to keep up with the way students are choosing to learn today.

Christensen et al. (2010) believe that technology is disrupting the education system and in the near future teachers will take on a different role in the classroom. Teachers will become guides or advisors in the learning process and help students learn using different forms of technology. The use of technology coupled with new approaches to teaching will force educators to use different types of assessments that will help educators connect with their students and develop more meaningful relationships.

Stephen Brookfield has an interesting view of assessment. In his book *The Skillful Teacher* (2006) he identifies several reflective practices where college students are provided tools for assessing their educators in order to determine how the educator can better help them learn. For instance, the Critical Incident Questionnaire (CIQ) asks students the following questions:

- At what moment in class this week did you feel most engaged with what was happening?
- At what moment in class this week were you most distanced from what was happening?
- What action that anyone (teacher or student) took this week did you find most affirming or helpful?
- What action that anyone took this week did you find most puzzling or confusing?
- What about the class this week surprised you the most? (pp. 42–43)

He uses this tool on a routine basis during his courses to better understand what students are experiencing in his classes, as well as to improve upon his teaching practices to help them learn more effectively. He mentions that this tool has improved his teaching, allowing him to become a more effective educator, and allowing him to change his practices midstream while the course is still in session, which helps maximize student learning.

Imagine if high school and college educators across the country were required to use this assessment tool! What would students say about their classes and their teachers? Would this create change in classroom teaching practices? Would students suggest changing class formats to include less lecturing and less standardized testing? I think so!

If teachers were to take the risk of allowing students to do the CIQ and then adjust their practices according to student input, classrooms would look very different. This, however, would be difficult for teachers who are unwilling to relinquish some power to their students. Educators would have to allow students the freedom to take the CIQ, listen to what students say about their teaching, and then change their teaching according to the feedback. The use of this tool could help improve teaching practices and ultimately enhance student learning, but unfortunately intimidated teachers will probably never use this tool.

Students ought to consider starting a peaceful intellectual revolution demanding more engaging teaching methods that allow them to be active participants in the learning process. They should be allowed to regain their curiosity for learning and demand more freedom to explore ideas that are meaningful and relevant to their lives. Students should be provided with authentic learning and have open honest discussions in their classrooms about how they learn best and what they want to learn.

What would students want to change in their classrooms? They would probably want classrooms to be more engaging and allow them more freedom to learn things that they are interested in, as opposed to learning the curriculum standards in a lockstep fashion. Currently, students have no freedom in deciding anything about what goes on in the classroom. Most of what students learn in high school is dictated by NCLB, and there is little time available for exploring topics in depth. Students would probably also want more hands-on learning and opportunities to learn useful skills.

There have been many times in my life when I have talked with people who, after finding out I am a professor, tell me that they were not very good students in high school or college. I often ask them why, and they tell me that they were not good at taking tests but were better at hands-on learning—not book learning. My hunch is that most people would agree that they are hands-on learners because life demands it. If educators could include more hand-on learning and application of information, a greater number of students would excel in their learning.

New schools are being developed, especially within the charter school movement; however, many of these schools are offering more of the same. These charter schools believe more of the same is good, and so they offer longer classes, longer days, and longer school years. They are succeeding at raising test scores and closing the achievement gap, but once again, students are not learning skills that are needed to succeed in life.

Take a minute right now to reflect back on your own learning when you were in high school or pursuing an undergraduate degree. What do you remember about the content of your courses? Probably not much.

I was a biology major in college but remember very little about the content. I had a difficult time deciding on a major and thought that biology courses such as botany, ecology, and zoology would get me outside the classroom doing hands-on learning, but I was wrong. Most of my courses consisted of lectures and short labs in the laboratory rooms. One thing I do remember was reading about timber wolves in an ecology class and thinking how interesting it would be to do research on this animal. The next semester I applied for a job trapping timber wolves and was hired by the U.S. Fish and Wildlife Service.

I can't tell you much about the biology books I read during my college years, but I can tell you plenty about the research I conducted while trapping wolves in northern Minnesota, and that was over thirty years ago. Hands-on problem solving was a daily routine in my life when I was working as a biological technician.

How to set traps, where to set traps, how to dart and radio collar animals, where the wolf pack territories were located, what they were eating, how they hunted, and many other questions like these were raised every day. The researchers were constantly thinking of ideas, testing them out, and reflecting on how to improve upon them. We were not reading textbooks; we were doing the things that people write about in textbooks.

The sole purpose of education is not to memorize the bold print found in textbooks; the purpose should be to apply the bold print and use this information to solve problems. Students do not need more textbook information to remember, because they will forget it all shortly after the test anyway. If retention is a goal of education, then hands-on application, which helps us learn problem-solving skills, is the process needed to help students retain information.

Allowing students to apply information turns them into researchers attempting to discover knowledge. This type of learning process takes on a whole different dimension. Students are typically motivated to learn using this process because they are attempting to find solutions to problems. With this process students are not memorizing information that has already been discovered; they are looking into the future and trying to discover their own answers to problems. One can look backward in time at what has already been discovered, or one can be given a problem that leads out into the future and attempts to discover the unknown. The latter process creates a challenge for students, which motivates them to inquire and explore, in attempts to discover knowledge.

New types of schools are being created that are clearly helping students develop important life skills and are pushing mainstream education to examine new teaching practices and techniques. EdVisions Inc. is an example of an organization that has created multiple schools based on innovative teaching practices that focus on hands-on learning and application of information. These schools are truly unique and produce alumni who are extraordinarily self-confident and self-directed.

I have been conducting research on project-based learning (PBL) and PBL schools for several years and have come to a clear conclusion that students who attend these schools have an advantage over their traditional counterparts when it comes to life skills. Two schools where I have conducted research are Minnesota New Country School (MNCS) and Avalon Charter School. I surveyed alumni from these schools and asked them questions about what they were learning and had them rank different academic and life skills they learned while attending these schools. Table 2.1 is a list of skills adapted from the SCANS report that I asked them to rank.

At both schools students ranked the life skills extremely high, whereas academic skills were much lower. When combining good and excellent rankings, creativity, finding information, problem solving, and learning how to learn were near or above 90 percent at MNCS (Wurdinger & Rudolph, 2009). The combined good and excellent rankings at Avalon Charter School were very similar (Wurdinger & Enloe, 2011). When combining good and excellent rankings at Avalon, all but one life skill (being a team player) were ranked in the mideighties to midnineties. This is perhaps due to the fact that students identify projects that are of their own interest, and others may not be interested in working on these projects together.

Academic skills, on the other hand, were ranked much lower. The four skills with the lowest scores at MNCS included test taking (33 percent), note taking (39 percent), math (58 percent), and writing (61 percent). Fifty percent of the alumni who answered our survey graduated from an

Table 2.1.   Skill Types

Academic Skills	Life Skills
Writing	Creativity
Math	Problem Solving
Verbal	Decision Making
Listening	Time Management
Study Skills	Finding Information
Note Taking Skills	Learning How to Learn
Test Taking Skills	Responsibility
	Team Player

undergraduate institution, which is considerably higher than the national average of 39 percent (National Center for Public Policy and Higher Education, 2006). These academic skills seem fairly important to college success, yet the MNCS students were able to navigate their way through a four-year degree in spite of these low rankings.

Perhaps this is due to their high levels of life skills. Learning how to find information, solve problems, and how to be a self-directed learner allowed them to navigate their way through a four-year college degree in spite of their lower levels of academic skills. This suggests that learning life skills may be more important than learning specific academic skills like how to take notes and how to take tests.

Something unique is going on at these schools, which should be embraced by traditional mainstream schools. Students at these schools actually enjoy going to school and are excited about their learning. Here are a few comments made by students from Avalon Charter School:

- I feel Avalon gave me the ability to view the world in a lens that is not entirely black and white; I am continually very grateful for Avalon for giving me skills to live in community, to see the world holistically, to be friends with people not exactly like me, and to understand that grades and test scores are not the most important things in life.
- Avalon gave me advantages in life by igniting my passion for learning so that even when I'm not in school, I am continually searching for ways to better my life and keep myself an active member of community.
- Avalon helped teach me the value of community; Avalon taught me to find my goals and dreams and run after them.
- I see learning and school as an enjoyable challenge and am more motivated to continue school than some of my peers.
- Self-reliance and independence allow me to direct my life where I want to go with less outside support.
- I understand and respect community; I know how to deal with people from all sorts of backgrounds (Wurdinger & Enloe, 2011).

At the philosophical core of EdVisions' schools is the teaching approach. Without this approach, learning would look very different. The teachers believe in this approach because they see students change over time and see that students are learning more than academic content; they are learning how to learn.

One of the key aspects to this approach is freedom. Teachers must provide students with freedom to make mistakes; otherwise it won't work. Freedom is critical in allowing students to learn how to be responsible, how to organize their projects, how to take responsibility for their actions, and how to become self-directed learners.

Teaching practices must change if we are to eliminate boredom and apathy in our high schools and colleges. It is time to move away from teaching to the test via the lecture format and start teaching important life skills that will motivate students to learn.

Chapter Three

Moving from
Memorization to Life Skills

Educators are constrained by the current assessment system, which forces them to teach to the test. The classroom culture that is created from this situation forces students to learn through a process of memorization. This process strips them of their natural tendencies. People enjoy freedom to explore their ideas; they like to learn by doing, to be engaged mentally as well as physically, and they are innately creative and curious.

The learning process is dependent upon what teaching method is used, and using more dynamic teaching approaches will help them learn by being actively engaged in the learning process. If educators were free from using standardized high-stakes tests as the primary way to assess students, they could change their practices and allow students to become more engaged in their learning.

A LESSON FROM EXTRACURRICULAR ACTIVITIES

Teaching approaches used in extracurricular activities are very different from direct instruction, which is typically used in many classroom settings. The educators overseeing extracurricular activities often demonstrate skills, and participants get to practice them as often as they like. Students are learning by doing, and the evaluation process as to whether students are improving upon their skill levels is observable, and usually obvious to coaches, club directors, and peers.

The benefits from participating in extracurricular activities include things like teamwork, time management, self-motivation, organization, communication, and research skills (Gould & Carson, 2008; Lawhorn,

2008). Students enjoy these activities because they learn technical skills associated with them, but they also learn life skills such as self-discipline and responsibility.

For example, working for the yearbook club allows students to learn technical skills such as writing and computer graphics, but students also learn how to communicate their ideas and collaborate with peers on their yearbook projects. Students are often more interested in participating in extracurricular activities than they are in their academic classes. Why is this?

Perhaps students are more interested in sports and other extracurricular activities because they are involved in hands-on activities with their peers working toward a common goal. They are performing certain skills and are able to see themselves improve over time. This process is entirely different from their academic life. Academic learning is primarily cerebral, requiring them to sit passively, listen, and remember information.

With extracurricular activities they get to do things. They get to use their hands and bodies to practice skills. They get to create, design, and build things. They get to practice skills and observe these skills improve over time. They get to socialize, interact, and communicate with the other members involved in the activity, without being given a letter grade.

Extracurricular activities such as sports might be the primary reason why U.S. students rank number one in self-confidence in the world (Duncan, 2010) yet rank much lower in academics. Sports are extremely popular in the United States and often seem to take precedence over academics. For example, parents and fans fill the bleachers at games; newspapers cover numerous high school, college, and professional sporting events on a daily basis; and at award banquets coaches hand out numerous awards that make students feel highly accomplished in their sport. Students' educational milestones are not nearly as publicized or popular as sporting accomplishments. Without sports, students' self-confidence might also be ranked lower than in other countries.

When I was in college I participated in an outing club and learned skills associated with rock climbing, backpacking, and winter camping. I learned about how to use the equipment, and all the safety procedures associated with these activities. I developed a high level of skill in these activities and eventually became one of the instructors for the club. I learned not only the technical skills, but also how to teach the skills.

I also learned life skills, such as how to be a better communicator, how to be an effective team member, and how to resolve conflict in groups. This club provided me with numerous opportunities to learn skills, which inspired me to continue learning, and essentially kept me from dropping out of college.

Educators need to take some of the principles associated with extracurricular activities and apply them to academia. Educators need to make academics more exciting by focusing on skill development. Some may ask how you would do this in a history or math class, and my answer is simple. Turn these subjects into skills that students can practice.

Educators need to look at academics through a different lens. Students should be practicing skills in all their subjects, allowing them to learn by doing. Teachers should allow students to experience academic subjects by letting them be active participants.

In the May/June 2011 issue of *American Teacher* there is an article that discusses linking school with after-school activities. The article states that after-school-project learning opportunities should "differ from regular school because projects can suffer when time must be tightly controlled; provide opportunities to tap students' interests; engage children in working collaboratively; provide a real world context in which to apply academic content; move students towards a goal; let them relax, unwind, and be less formal; build success and pride; help kids see the practical uses for whatever they are studying; and provide more choices than students get during the regular school day" (Project learning links school with "after school," 2011, p. 4). The article suggests that this is something that should occur after school as extracurricular activities, but if project learning actually does all these things, then why shouldn't it be used in all classes all day long?

Project learning could engage students in their learning in all subjects. Imagine if students could practice life skills while working on projects in all their classes, and could ask as many questions as they liked while practicing these skills as often as they liked to develop higher levels of proficiency. This learning process would allow students to experience things firsthand, as opposed to reading about them in textbooks. Unfortunately, in the current academic system, students are given information for tests, are not allowed to talk with peers or teachers when taking tests, and are penalized for wrong answers.

Educators need to give students opportunities to participate in activities, projects, and experiences so they can practice skills. Yes, activities, projects, and experiences take more time, but this allows for deeper learning, which inspires and motivates students. The learning is rich. Students could learn useful skills that they can carry with them after they graduate that have a lasting effect on their lives. Certain teaching approaches that can be used in classroom settings provide students with opportunities to practice skills and allow them to be actively involved in the learning process.

TEACHING APPROACHES THAT PROMOTE SKILL DEVELOPMENT

Five innovative teaching approaches that engage students in their learning and promote skill development are challenge-based learning, project-based learning, collaborative learning, problem-based learning, and service learning. These approaches are practical for classroom learning environments and can be implemented in any subject area. They are beginning to help educators step outside the confines of traditional education and are creating new learning environments that are changing the way students, educators, and administrators view the learning process.

Each approach begins by centering on students embracing situations where they are in control of what they learn, which in turn creates excitement and enthusiasm in students. Underlying principles of these approaches include hands-on learning, using a problem-solving process, addressing real-world problems, encouraging student interaction with each other and the content, engaging in direct experiences, using multiple subjects to enhance interdisciplinary learning, and skill development.

These principles are integral to experiential learning and are used in different proportions in these teaching approaches. For instance, project-based learning has a strong hands-on component because students are using their hands to design and construct products, whereas problem-based learning focuses more on having students undergo a problem-solving process where students work in small groups discussing and creating a plan to solve a real-life problem. Some of these teaching approaches may rely more heavily on one principle, whereas alternative approaches rely more heavily on others, but they all help students develop important life skills.

Although these teaching approaches have been implemented with all subject areas, certain ones lend themselves more readily to certain subjects. Project-based learning, for example, has been used in art, science, family and consumer sciences, and technology education because students in these disciplines often create artworks, perform experiments, bake food, and construct things from metal and wood.

Subjects that are less apt to use one of these approaches are history, philosophy, and math, where the focus tends to be on learning dates, theories, and equations. Problem-based learning might be a better method for these classical disciplines because problems can easily be identified and created within each of these subjects.

For example, a history problem could focus on key factors of how wars were started and how they could have been prevented; a philosophy problem could focus on ethical case studies and how people decide what is right and wrong; and a math problem could focus on how to use certain math formulas to solve real-life problems. Problems can be found everywhere in these subjects; it just takes a little creativity to design them so they are relevant to the learners.

These approaches have significant bodies of literature devoted to explaining theories and techniques that can help educators create more exciting classrooms by motivating students to learn on their own. There are even professional organizations that host conferences and workshops to help educators integrate these approaches into their schools and classrooms.

All of these approaches help students learn important life skills because they require students to work together creating projects and solving problems that have relevance to them, their peers, and often their community. They also provide students opportunities to work in teams, manage their time, be responsible for completing their tasks, communicate with peers, and present their ideas to classmates and teachers.

When students are engaged in hands-on projects with classmates, they have to test out their ideas, which requires critical-thinking and problem-solving skills, as well as communication with their peers. There is no way students can avoid practicing life skills when educators use these teaching approaches.

The amount of attention these approaches are receiving continues to increase, and there appears to be a growing movement to use them in both high school and college classrooms. They require time to implement correctly, but they are rewarding, especially when students become self-directed learners. A brief explanation of each approach is provided so educators can determine which approach or approaches may best fit their classroom situation.

The first four approaches can be implemented in classroom settings; however, students may need to gather resources outside the classroom at various times. Much of the up-front work with service learning, the last approach, may also be done in the classroom; however, it will require students to do the actual service project outside the classroom.

Challenge-Based Learning

Challenge-based learning is a new approach developed by a team of educators from Apple Inc. that was launched in December 2008 (Johnson, Smith, Smythe, & Varon, 2009). The idea behind this approach stems from a combination of project-based learning and inquiry learning where students address real-world problems that lead to action and solutions to these problems.

The beginning phases of the framework, which consist of the Big Idea, Essential Question, and the Challenge, are teacher directed because the teacher needs to consider how to cover state standards through these elements. Once the educator has identified the Big Idea, Essential Question, and the Challenge, the students are broken into teams and begin the process of finding solutions to the Challenge.

As students begin this process they will develop guiding questions, guiding activities, and guiding resources. Guiding questions, activities, and resources will help keep them focused and allow different team members to tackle different parts of the Challenge. The action phase of the process is creating a realistic solution and carrying it through to determine whether or not it works.

The assessment is performance based in that students must create some sort of document such as an iMovie or blog that might include photographs, animation, audio clips, or video clips and present them to the class. Educators evaluate both the product that is created as well as the presentation of the material using rubrics. Figure 3.1 shows how the process flows from one phase to the next and was adapted from "Challenge-Based Learning: An Approach for Our Time" (Johnson et al., 2009).

The challenge must be relevant to students and have a realistic solution that students can accomplish within a given time frame. Some challenges are bigger and may require a full semester of work to complete, whereas others are smaller and may only require a couple of class periods to finish.

Jose Garcia, a science teacher at the Greene County Middle School in North Carolina, who received the Apple Distinguished Educator Award in 2009 and was the Teacher of the Year in his school and county in 2008–2009, has been using this approach since 2008. While talking to him, he gave me an example of how his middle school students work their way through the process.

One lesson was on the human body, which was the Big Idea. The Essential Question was, how do the systems of the human body function together to support life? And the Challenge was for students to create a

BIG IDEAS

ESSENTIAL QUESTION

THE CHALLENGE

GUIDING QUESTIONS GUIDING ACTIVITIES GUIDING RESOURCES

SOLUTION-ACTION

ASSESSMENT

PUBLISHING—STUDENT SAMPLES PUBLISHING—STUDENT REFLECTION

Figure 3.1. Challenge-Based Learning Process

podcast with four pieces of quality information on one of the human body systems, which included skeletal, circulatory, muscular, or digestive. Students who chose to do their podcast on the skeletal system needed to first do research on how the skeletal system works, and after they collected four pieces of quality information, they would have to video themselves with their props and explain how the system functions in relation to the Essential Question.

Examples of guiding questions for the students who chose the skeletal system included, What are the systems of the human body? What are the functions of each of these systems? How do you keep your bones strong? What are two main types of joints? and What are the differences between fractures, dislocations, and sprains? For a guiding activity, Jose had students make piñatas that looked like the systems they chose for their challenge. Guiding Resources for their project included online research using university libraries, government websites, and netTrekker.com.

The Solution/Action phase of the process is the podcast presentation, and Jose uses rubrics to evaluate students' presentation, as well as their ability to use technology and corollary projects such as the piñata. Typically, students publish their podcast on TeacherTube, Wikispaces, or Xtranormal.

Jose also told me about some of the details of the process. He breaks students into groups of four and has each student be responsible for specific tasks while working through the process. Students apply pressure on each other if one is not putting forth the needed effort to produce a quality podcast. Thinking Maps are used for students to brainstorm ideas for their podcast, and this is where they begin thinking about what type of information they need to research to produce the podcast (J. Garcia, personal communication, April 7, 2011).

His entire curriculum for grades 6–8 has been converted to this approach, and he does not use books, which makes it a paperless class. He is able to use this approach within fifty-five-minute class periods. Educators who use this process need to become familiar with the 21st Century Skills that focus on students learning life skills like problem solving and creativity.

Challenge-based-learning classrooms allow educators to provide students with more one-on-one attention on a daily basis, which allows students to continue moving forward with their learning, and educators act as guides to the learning process rather than keepers of knowledge. Students are assessed continually throughout the entire process, and adjustments can be made at any time for each individual student.

I could sense his enthusiasm as we talked by his willingness to go into specific detail about how he engages students in this process. Some of the top reasons why he likes using this approach include that it improves motivation and engagement; it teaches important life skills such as time management, responsibility, and self-directed learning; classroom management is easier because students are engaged in the learning; teachers are able to cover more standards in a shorter amount of time; and students do better on state tests. As a side note, Jose has a 98 percent passing rate in his classes, and his state-mandated end-of-grade (EOG) test scores have gone from the midthirties to the midfifties in three years.

Apple Inc. was interested in the effectiveness of this approach, so it piloted the program with six schools in the fall of 2008, ranging in size and demographics. They were interested in determining whether this approach could be beneficial to small and large schools, in both rural and urban areas. School locations included Manor, Texas; O'Neill, Nebraska; Mooresville, North Carolina; Pratt, Kansas; Hayward, California; and Honolulu, Hawaii. These schools had a wide range of demographics.

Research was conducted on students, faculty, and administrators while these schools were implementing this approach. The research was qualitative in nature and consisted mostly of written and video journals from all participants. Pre and post data were collected on their views of this approach. The results were extremely positive.

Of the 321 students, 97 percent "found the experience worthwhile," and 73 percent of the teachers said they were able to engage all their students in the class (Johnson et al., 2009, p. 4).

This approach is tied to the 21st Century Skills and has shown promising results in helping students learn these skills, which include "critical thinking and problem solving, communication, creativity, media literacy, contextual learning, leadership, ethics, accountability, adaptability, responsibility, self direction, and social responsibility" (Johnson et al., 2009, p. 15). Although this approach is relatively new, it has tremendous potential. Numerous educators around the country are beginning to use this approach because it motivates students and allows them to take control of their own learning.

Project-Based Learning

Project-based learning (PBL) has been defined as "a teaching method where teachers guide students through a problem solving process which includes identifying a problem, developing a plan, testing the plan against reality, and reflecting on the plan while in the process of designing and completing a project" (Wurdinger, Haar, Hugg, & Bezon, 2007, p. 151). Multiple research studies across North America suggest that project-based learning motivates students to learn because it taps into their interests and changes their attitudes about school (Blumenfeld et al., 1991; Grant & Branch, 2005; Levine, 2002; Littky & Grabelle, 2004; Newell, 2003; Thomas, Enloe, & Newell, 2005).

With this teaching approach students create and produce projects. For instance, students might build a birdhouse, design a web page, or create a learning portfolio as a project. Some teachers are more teacher directed with this approach and identify the projects ahead of time, whereas other teachers use a student-centered approach and allow students to create their own projects.

Organizations such as the Buck Institute for Education and Edutopia provide numerous resources that help educators integrate PBL into their curriculums. Much of their focus, however, is on how to integrate PBL into mainstream public schools that are bound to the traditional structures such as compartmentalized subject matter, short class periods, and student achievement that is based on test scores. While this is definitely a step in the right direction, these structures often promote a teacher-directed approach where the teacher determines what project the student will complete, which does not necessarily promote student interest.

EdVisions Inc. is another leading organization that helps schools integrate project-based learning in their curriculums; however, their approach is unique. Their focus is student centered, where students choose and develop their own projects, which increases motivation to learn. Their flagship school is called Minnesota New Country School (MNCS), which is located in Henderson, Minnesota.

In a conversation with Jim Wartman, one of the lead teachers at this school, he explained to me the importance of using a student-centered philosophy with this approach. He said, "When students are creating their own projects they take more ownership in their learning, and they learn how to become self-directed learners. When teachers are directing the process there tends to be less student interest in the project, and the learning often requires less problem solving because teachers often demonstrate how to create the project in a prescriptive fashion" (J. Wartman, personal communication, March 2, 2011). He believes students should be allowed to make mistakes because that is how we learn, and teachers should act as guides to the learning process and allow students to take responsibility for their learning.

He also mentioned that the true value in this approach is that over time students switch their thinking and realize that they are responsible for their own learning, especially those students who come from traditional school settings where teachers direct the learning process and students are forced to listen to teachers and memorize information. He mentioned that this process does not happen right away, and educators have to be patient with students engaged in project-based learning. But if the educator stays the course, most students will learn how to become self-directed learners.

On one of my first trips to visit MNCS, I immediately noticed that the school looks much different from a traditional high school classroom. The main room is large without walls and contains several clusters of computers. Each cluster or pod has ten to twelve computers in a semicircle with a workstation desk. The room looks more like a business office than a classroom. Many students are busy working on their computers, while others are building and constructing things in some of the other larger rooms.

One room contains several pieces of woodworking machinery, and there were a number of wood duck boxes that the students had built up against the wall. One of the teachers, called advisors, told me they would hang them on trees at a local nature center where they frequently visited to do research projects. Another room is a greenhouse with various carnivorous plants that students do research on and several fish tanks filled with different types of fish that are also being used for research.

I spoke to several students and found one of them building a full-size Smart Board for the school. He explained to me how he was using laser technology to build it into the board. Another student was building a water fountain for the school, and another explained that he was working on designing computer software programs.

Students were extremely interested in their own projects and were excited to explain to me intricate details of their projects. It did not take me long to realize that these students were very motivated about learning because they were working on projects that they were interested in and that were relevant to their lives because they will integrate them into the school or community where fellow students will have access to them.

At MNCS, project-based learning is at the heart of the curriculum. Students create their own projects and are assessed on their learning primarily during the presentation phase of the project process. If the team believes the student reached a certain level of proficiency, then they sign off on the project, and the student moves on to the next project. If not, the student must continue to work on the project and present it again to the team.

Much of the time students work alone on their own projects, primarily because of their own specific interests; however, students are allowed to collaborate when they have similar interests in a project. Projects are broad ranging and have included things like designing museums, developing software programs, creating videos and movies, and creating documentaries through pictures (Newell, 2003). Depending upon their complexity, these projects may take a few days or several months to complete. When students finish a project, they demonstrate their level of understanding by doing a presentation for their advisory group, which consists of peers, advisors, community members, and parents. After the presentation, advisors and students sit down together and discuss what state curriculum standards have been met and how many credits they will receive for their work.

In the state of Minnesota, students must complete all of the state standards, so students at EdVisions' schools are provided a copy of the standards when they enroll and are asked to be mindful of how they might complete these standards through their projects. Students move through this process at their own pace and finish their high school education when they have met all the mandatory state standards. Advisors work closely with students to make sure that all standards have been addressed through their project work. Some students graduate earlier than their traditional counterparts, and others graduate later.

In 2006, WestEd was commissioned to conduct research for the U.S. Department of Education on charter schools that were closing the achievement gap. The publication that resulted from this research is titled "Charter High Schools Closing the Achievement Gap" (U.S. Department of Education, 2006). Researchers found that MNCS was one of the top eight charter schools in the nation in closing the achievement gap. In 2005, MNCS had 24 percent of their students qualify for special education services, compared to 12 percent at the neighboring high school in LeSueur Henderson called the LeSueur Henderson Secondary School (LHSS). Even though MNCS had higher numbers of special education students, they outperformed LHSS, scoring 80 percent proficiency in math, compared with 73 percent for LHSS students. In addition, MNCS students' average ACT scores were 23.3, compared with a national average of 20.9 (p. 46).

The project process from beginning to end includes writing a project proposal, getting approval from the advisor, presenting the proposal to the proposal team, working on the project until it is completed, meeting with the proposal team to determine what standards have been met, and presenting the project to the proposal team. Figure 3.2 provides more detail on how students walk through the project process at MNCS.

Project Foundry is an online software program used at MNCS that helps students walk through their projects in a structured fashion and allows advisors to track students' progress. The software program provides a variety of forms that students fill out as they reach certain steps in the project process. It also helps determine what standards and benchmarks are met with each project.

When project-based learning is less teacher directed and more student centered, students learn to tap into their interests and create projects that are relevant to them. They learn skills such as how to be self-directed, time management, responsibility, organization, and public speaking. They also learn how to problem solve because projects require a process of trial and error. Students try something, and if it does not work, they must think of a different plan and try it again. They find solutions through a process of thinking and doing, and they learn to solve problems by testing out their ideas against reality.

This approach can be used in classroom settings, but like the other approaches mentioned in this chapter, students must be given time to research and collect information that they need to complete their projects. This might require students to make phone calls, make visits to places in the community, or spend time in the library or computer lab. They will need some freedom to collect necessary information needed to complete their projects.

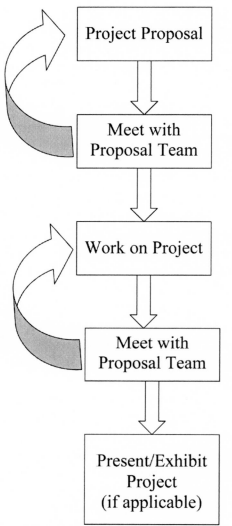

Brainstorm Ideas
- Create and Revise Project Proposal on Project Foundry
- **Advisor says "Looks Good"**
- **Have Parent Sign Proposal Form and Give to Advisor**

- Discuss Ideas and Finalize Plans With Team
- **Proposal Team Signs Project Proposal**

- Research, Create, Etc…
- Log Time Everyday on PF
- Write Project Reflection
- **Give to Advisor:**
  - **Project Reflection**
  - **List of Resources**
  - **Timelogs**

- Discuss Project With Team
- Ask For Credit and Standards
- **Team Assigns Credit and Standards**

- Pre-present to Advisor/Team
- Complete Presentation/Exhibit Form
- Attend Presentation Night

Figure 3.2. Project-Based Learning Process
Adapted from Colin O'Brien, Minnesota New Country School.

Collaborative/Cooperative Learning

Collaborative and cooperative learning are two very similar approaches that attempt to get students talking in the classroom. Collaborative learning provides students with more freedom to be self-directed in the learning process and is therefore associated more with college classrooms;

whereas cooperative learning is associated with high school classrooms because it relies on the educator to provide more structure and direction in the learning process (Bruffee, 1995).

With both approaches, students work in pairs or small groups to find solutions to problems and questions posed by the educator. Discussion techniques include things like interviews, role-playing, simulations, debates, teaching episodes, and small-group problem-solving exercises. Collaborative and cooperative learning are similar enough that I will use the term *collaborative learning* to mean both collaborative and cooperative learning in the remainder of this section.

In an attempt to encourage more educators to use collaborative learning, authors such as Barkley, Cross, and Howell Major (2005) and Brookfield and Preskill (2005) describe ways to intentionally integrate techniques that promote meaningful discussion in the classroom. Typically, the class format includes breaking into small groups or pairs to discuss a predetermined question or questions, record the information, and provide the large class with a report of the findings from the small-group discussion. For example, students could be broken into groups of four and asked to discuss the advantages and disadvantages of nuclear energy, record the information they talk about in their group, and provide a verbal report of their findings to the large class.

The primary goal of using collaborative learning techniques, while working in small groups, is to get students talking in the classroom. When students are engaged in discussion it provides them an opportunity to express their ideas and think critically about how to solve problems. Below is a sample of collaborative learning techniques taken from Barkley, Cross, and Howell Major (2005) with explanations for each:

Think-Pair-Share: The educator presents the class with a question that does not have one correct answer. For example, what are some of the most pressing problems our school currently faces? Students are given a minute or two to think about the question and are asked to share their ideas with a partner. After several minutes of sharing their ideas, students report their ideas to the whole class.

Critical Debate: A debate question is identified, such as, are standardized tests the best way to measure intelligence? Students are asked to create two groups, one that will take the yes side and one that will take the no side. Once the groups have been formed, students are asked to argue the opposing side. They are given time to create their arguments, and then each group is given a certain amount of time to present their arguments. A large-group discussion follows after the debate is over.

Fishbowl: An inner and outer circle is created and a question is posed to the inner circle. The inner circle discusses the question verbally, while the outer circle records notes on the discussion. After several minutes of discussion the students in the outer circle provide a report on what they heard and a large-group discussion with all students follows.

Jigsaw: This is a peer-teaching technique where the teaching students have been identified ahead of time and are responsible for teaching the others about an assigned topic. Students are broken into small groups, and one of the members of the group is the designated teaching student. Each teaching student teaches the others about a topic that they have been given the prior class period. For example, in a science class one student could be asked to teach the differences between meiosis and mitosis, whereas another could be asked to teach others the difference between deciduous and coniferous trees. Every five minutes students are asked to rotate to another group, which allows the teaching students to teach the topic several times, helping to solidify the learning.

Peer Editing: Two or three students are asked to write a formal paper together. They identify the pieces they would like to write and then need to blend the two or three pieces of writing together. Once the paper is completed they take turns revising and editing the whole paper.

The primary focus of collaborative learning techniques is to create discussion in the classroom. The pitfall with these techniques is that students do not usually get a chance to test out their ideas against reality to see if they work. The techniques generate discussion and help students learn to think critically, but students typically do not go through a trial-and-error process like they would with other teaching approaches. Students discuss ideas and create plans for solutions, but due to time constraints, they are often not allowed opportunities to carry out the plans to see if they will work. When the trial-and-error process is eliminated, students may miss out on learning valuable problem-solving skills.

These techniques emphasize the importance of learning skills such as communication, time management, public speaking, and being a team player. They are designed to occur in classrooms where time is limited, and whether working in pairs or in groups, the ultimate goal is to engage students in learning through discussion.

Problem-Based Learning

Problem-based learning focuses on having students undergo a problem-solving process and includes working together in small groups to find solutions. The roots of problem-based learning stem back to the field of medical education at McMaster University in Ontario, Canada, when they began using it in 1969 as an alternative approach to train doctors in analyzing medical problems (Ramsey & Sorel, 2007). Barrows and Tamblyn (1980), two of the pioneers of problem-based learning, defined it as "the learning that results from the process of working toward the understanding or resolution of a problem" (p. 18). More recently, it has been defined as a process where "students formulate and pursue their own learning objectives by researching a situation, developing appropriate questions, and producing their own solution to a problem" (Maxwell, Mergendoller, & Bellisimo, 2005, p. 316).

Delisle (1997) identified a four-step process that includes ideas, facts, learning issues, and an action plan. In small groups, students are given a problem and asked to discuss their understanding of the problem. Students do not move to the "ideas" step until they all have an understanding of the problem. The idea phase involves making a list of all the ideas they have for potential solutions to the problem.

Once they have identified a number of ideas, they make a list of all the facts they know about the problem. Next, they make another list of all the learning issues that they will need to research in order to move forward to make an action plan. Learning issues are things they don't know but will need to know in order to create an action plan.

The learning issues step usually requires a longer time frame than the previous steps. Students must gather information by doing research, which might require a trip to a library or contacting individuals who may know the answers to their questions. After they have acquired the information about what they don't know, they create an action plan to solve the problem. The action plan step may also require extra time to complete because students tend to alter the plan as they discuss their potential solutions.

In a history class, for example, students could be given a problem of how the local museum could create an exhibit that would provide information on the history of their town. If working as one large group, they would first make a list of ideas on what an exhibit might look like and possible things that should be included in the exhibit. This would require having a discussion on what students know about exhibits and what they know about the history of their town.

Once they have created a list of ideas, they would make a list of all the things they know. They might know and be able to describe an exhibit from previous experiences they have had in museums. They might also know some local history from the books they have read or from speaking to their grandparents and relatives.

Next, they would make a list of the things they don't know. This might include facts such as the year the town was founded, names of the early settlers in the area, the first buildings constructed in the town, the names of the individuals who made significant impacts on the town, and the names and types of early businesses that had an impact. During this step in the process, students might visit the museum to find out what they already have on the history of the town and what other information or artifacts they would like to include in an exhibit.

The next step is to identify the learning issues. This step often entails students splitting up the learning issues so that each student is responsible for collecting needed information to create the action plan. Once they have collected their information, students report their learning issues back to the group. The last step would be to create an action plan for the museum to create the exhibit. Table 3.1 is an example of how students would walk through the problem-based learning process.

Table 3.1.   Problem-Based Learning Process

Ideas	Facts	Learning Issues	Action Plan
Things to include in the museum exhibit, such as pictures and artifacts.	Names of early pioneers and settlers who founded the town. Names of individuals who had a significant impact on the town. Unique feature of the town.	How big is the space of the exhibit? What information should be included in the space? What unique features should be included?	Work with the local museum to create the exhibit. Where should artifacts be placed in the exhibit space?

With this approach students must conduct research, communicate their ideas effectively, be responsible for collecting information, and report back to the group. This requires skills such as problem solving, communication, responsibility, collaboration, and organization. The overall process requires students to think and to analyze problems that they might encounter in real-life situations. This approach is used in classroom settings but requires students to spend some time in the library or computer lab researching and collecting information.

Service Learning

Service learning is an approach that blends learning with providing a service to a community. Identifying a need is the first step, which is followed by creating an action plan to address this need. "Service Learning can be defined as a teaching method where guided or classroom learning is deepened through service to others in a process that provides structured time for reflection on the service experience and demonstration of the skills and knowledge acquired" (Kaye, 2004, p. 7).

According to Soslau and Yost (2007), service learning increases student achievement and motivation by eliciting real-world connections between book learning and the everyday lives of students. When students are actively engaged in service learning projects, they begin to take more ownership of their own learning, which increases their motivation to continue their learning.

By creating a link between school and the community, students become more invested, not only in their schoolwork, but in their community as well. Some of the benefits and reasons cited for adopting service learning in schools include helping students to become more active members of the community, increasing student knowledge and understanding of the community, meeting real community needs, and encouraging students' altruism and caring for others (Billing, 2000).

For example, students may see a need to help feed lower-income families in their community, so they can organize a food drive and work with the local food bank to deliver donations to families. Service could include an assignment such as interviewing the manager at the food bank about community needs and then publishing an article in the local paper. Service learning projects often provide greater depth to the learning experience. However, it is important to help students make connections between the service and the learning, because simply providing a service does not mean that the student is taking away any learning.

Many schools and universities are weaving service into their mission statements and formalizing a service learning component into requirements for graduation. Numerous benefits can be attributed to participating in service learning, including greater self-knowledge, increased personal efficacy, a better ability to work with others, a heightened feeling of being connected to a community, and closer ties between students and faculty (Eyler & Giles, 1999).

The learning process involves several steps, which include identifying a need in the community, making a plan to address the need, executing the plan, and reflecting on what was learned from the experience (Cress, Collier, & Reitenauer, 2005). Identifying a need may be a bit challenging. Educators need to consider the scope of the need and whether the class can accomplish the tasks required to complete the project. The need should be a real need in the community, something that when completed will help make the community a better place for people to live.

Once the need has been identified, students will need to create a plan to address the need. This can be done in one large group or smaller groups. Sometimes it is beneficial to break into smaller groups so that each group can address specific pieces that will need to be accomplished to complete the big project. Once the plan is developed, students must execute the plan and actually do the project. After the project is completed, students should reflect on their entire experience and discuss the learning outcomes that occurred.

For example, some of my students recently identified a need in the community, which focused on renovating and creating new curriculum stations at a local nature center. Students contacted the director and set up a meeting at the center. The center had been in disrepair for a few years after the local school district decided not to fund it any longer.

Students visited the nature center, had conversations with the director, and identified a list of ideas that could result in new learning stations at the center. Wall murals with plant and animal identification activities, squirrel obstacle courses, video and audio activities about birds and insects were a few of the ideas that were generated. Students broke into groups and began creating plans for these different stations and then began to identify specific tasks that individuals could work on before the next meeting session.

During the rest of the semester they worked on these projects and slowly completed them. Through the process they learned better communication skills, how to work in teams, how to be responsible for doing their individual tasks, and how to manage their time to complete the tasks. They also learned that it felt good to help their community provide a service that would educate young children to appreciate their natural environment. The project was such a success that some students continued to provide service to the nature center after the semester course had ended.

Service learning is more challenging to implement than the other approaches because it requires spending time away from school. Much of the work can be completed at school, but doing the project requires students to leave the school and be at the place where the project will occur. It also requires some upfront time on the educator's part. Educators must contact the community member and make arrangements for the project to occur.

All students should be involved in doing the project, so this might present a logistical problem for larger class sizes. This approach has tremendous potential for students to learn life skills because they must not only complete the project but they must also step outside the school and engage with community members to complete the project.

OUTCOMES WHEN USING THESE APPROACHES

One of the more obvious outcomes from using these approaches is that students begin to take ownership of their learning. They begin to understand what it means to be a self-directed learner. This does not happen overnight, but it does happen, and it becomes quite obvious in their behavior after using these approaches for a semester or two. The life skills they learn help them understand that they are in control of their own learning. It is through practicing and learning these types of skills that they become self-directed in their learning.

One of the outcomes for educators is that they must learn to take less control in the classroom; otherwise these approaches will not be as effective. Students must be allowed to experiment with their ideas and learn from their mistakes. Educators need to allow this problem-solving process to occur, realizing that students will not always find the correct solution on their first attempt. Too often educators step in and provide students with the answers when they get stuck, but this will not help them learn to solve problems.

With these approaches, educators must take a less visible role in the classroom, guiding students through the learning process by encouraging them to take risks and challenging them to learn from their mistakes. Students should be given more freedom to explore the learning process, and the educator's role is to provide resources and information, not answers, which will help students move forward with their own learning.

The educator's role is more like a facilitator, with the purpose founded in guiding students in designing meaningful learning experiences and allowing students time to complete and demonstrate their comprehension to an audience of peers. Educators are not the center of attention in the classroom; student learning is.

A different type of classroom culture is created when using these teaching approaches. Students become active participants with these teaching approaches and need to understand that a different culture combined with a set of expectations is a beneficial way to learn. Changing the classroom culture requires a change in the educator's role and the student's role, as well as a change in the classroom structure.

Students should not be confined to their chairs. Students need to experience their learning in a less directed way to fully benefit from these teaching approaches. To engage in their learning process, students need autonomy, which may include brainstorming ideas with peers, moving around the classroom to gather resources, and using technology to access information.

Research conducted by Vansteenkiste, Lens, and Deci (2006) suggests that students are more motivated to learn when they are allowed to choose their own activities and are provided with some autonomy in the classroom. Giving students some direction about the tasks to be completed and then freedom to pursue their learning will increase their level of motivation. Something as simple as rearranging classroom desks into circles or small pods, having them work in small groups, and having unlimited access to computer technology will help change the culture of the classroom.

An important consideration when using these innovative approaches is that they are not "all-or-nothing" strategies for classroom engagement. There will be times when certain material needs to be covered by the teacher in order for students to move forward in the learning process. With each of these approaches educators can have a large or a small role during the active phase of learning.

The most important underlying theme is that through these approaches students will become engaged in learning. Providing opportunities that allow for creativity, direct experience, and personal interpretation will not only engage students in their learning but will also promote a more humanistic approach to education.

RELEVANCE AND RIGOR BUILDS SKILLS

When students are engaged in learning experiences that are relevant, rigor usually follows. In many cases the rigor is self-imposed. They want to learn as much as possible and go more deeply into the topic because it has purpose and meaning to their lives. In such situations learning becomes more than just memorization because students want to test out their ideas against reality and apply the learning to their own lives. During this process they begin to learn skills such as how to be more effective problem solvers.

Oliver Zornow, an alumnus from Valley New School, which is a project-based charter school in Appleton, Wisconsin, told me about how his senior project launched him down his career path of international relations (personal communication, April 23, 2011). His senior project focused on global poverty where he did research on how to develop a primary school in Haiti.

He and some classmates raised money to visit Haiti, and when they visited, they learned about the local politics and the legalities of starting a primary school. Since then, he has started the school, which has approximately 197 students enrolled. The school consists of temporary structures, but he hopes that his nonprofit organization will be able to raise enough money to build a permanent school building. He spends much of his time traveling around the country doing fund-raising speeches to raise money for the school.

He also told me how his senior project helped him learn and build valuable research, time management, and communication skills. His senior project was relevant and meaningful, which fully engaged him in his learning and took him far beyond the classroom to test out his ideas. This has been an arduous journey for this young man, but through multiple trial-and-error attempts he is succeeding.

His initial project was relevant and became rigorous when he began the process of implementing his ideas by creating the school. He learned important skills during this journey, allowing him to become a more effective problem solver and communicator.

One other example of how relevance and rigor builds skills comes from a former graduate student who is a teacher at a local middle school. She created a contest for her students to determine what they believed was a relevant problem that needed to be fixed at their school. The students brainstormed a list of problems, and through a process of elimination they decided that the school needed more options for healthy snacks. They voted to create a healthy snack shop because they wanted alternatives to what was currently being offered to them at their school. Her class decided that they would create and run the shop.

This project created a number of challenges and problems, which students had to overcome as they worked toward the creation of the shop, requiring a fair amount of problem solving and collaboration. They learned how to create a plan and follow through with the development of the plan. They tested out their ideas at the school and learned through a trial-and-error process.

Students had to find out what kinds of foods were healthy and appealing to the student body, how much they should charge for these foods, where they would purchase the foods they would sell, how to create a schedule for working the snack shop, and what they would do with the proceeds. They had to test out their ideas when they began selling food to see how to run the shop and adjust their ideas as they proceeded. This project allowed students to learn skills like problem solving, organization, communication, and responsibility.

It also allowed them to learn how to run a small business, and how to take on responsibilities for doing tasks and completing them. This type of learning is more rigorous and meaningful because it has a direct impact on their lives. Students take ownership of their learning because it was their idea.

This project probably impacted their lives in other ways as well. For instance, they may have learned more about health and nutrition and changed their eating behaviors, or they may have learned more about the importance of effective communication when running a small business. These are the types of skills they need to learn in order to survive in today's world.

The process of completing this particular project required students to consider multiple topics. Students learned about nutrition, marketing, economics, communication, and business practices, which is an interdisciplinary approach to learning. In traditional classes, educators compartmentalize subject matter and tend to break down content into small bits and pieces in order to provide students with just the necessary information they need for tests. When students take on the challenge of creating a complex project or solving a complex problem, they need to take a broader perspective and consider a wide range of topics. Each topic creates its own set of problems to solve, and solving these problems creates a rigorous learning environment for students.

Activities that are of interest to students have the potential to transform their lives and lead to other learning experiences. Experiences like these can change lives when they lead out into the future and inspire students to learn new things and discover new knowledge. Rigor requires that students do something with information. They need to apply it by demonstrating what they know, or telling others what they know. Rigor requires students to show or tell others what they know and explain the details of the activity, project, or experience.

Rigor should result in invigoration, where students are excited about learning and are motivated to do work on their own. Students should not need external motivation such as a multiple-choice test to do their homework. They will be more excited about finding answers and solutions to problems when the learning has direct relevance to their lives.

As adults we experience rigor all the time because we are faced with problems every day that we must solve. Our jobs require us to be problem solvers, as does owning a house, or raising children. Managing a budget, fixing household items, building things, raising a family—these all require an enormous amount of problem solving. As adults we solve problems every day and become fairly proficient at this skill because we practice it routinely. Why not equip our students with skills like these prior to graduation so they know how to solve complex problems once they enter the work world?

We need to teach and assess students differently. Rather than assessing their book learning, we should be assessing not only their ability to apply information, but the skills they are learning while applying information. When educators use teaching approaches like the ones mentioned in this chapter, students apply information, and through this process they learn important skills. These approaches allow students to learn and practice skills such as problem solving, communication, public speaking, time management, and responsibility. The time has come to change not only our teaching approaches but our assessment system as well, so that students will become motivated, self-directed learners.

Chapter Four

Skills, Benchmarks, and Assessments

According to Dictionary.com, a skill is "the ability, coming from one's knowledge, practice, aptitude, etc., to do something well: Carpentry was one of his many skills." The operative words here are *do something well*. Students should be allowed to learn skills and practice them so they learn to do things well.

There are two types of skills students should be learning in high school and college: technical skills associated with specific subjects and life skills that can be applied to all subjects. Writing, speaking, painting, playing an instrument, computer graphics, carpentry, engine mechanics, sewing, and baking are examples of technical skills that may be learned in subjects such as English, public speaking, art, music, industrial arts, auto mechanics, and family and consumer sciences. Practicing technical skills provides students with opportunities to learn useful skills that require them to solve problems.

Learning a technical skill and doing it well entails practice, and individuals practice skills because they desire to reach higher levels of proficiency. Numerous trial-and-error attempts are part of the process of becoming better at a skill, and problem solving is inherent in this process. For instance, public speaking requires figuring out how to create a speech that flows in a logical sequence, playing an instrument requires figuring out how to play certain notes in the correct order to produce a song, computer graphics requires figuring out how to use software programs to create intended graphics, and carpentry requires figuring out correct dimensions and measurements as well as how to use equipment and tools to create products. Problem solving is a natural part of the process of learning technical skills.

Unfortunately, when budgets are tight, courses that teach technical skills such as art, music, industrial arts, auto mechanics, and family and consumer sciences are usually the first ones cut from high school curriculums. These courses are often viewed as being less academically rigorous than math, history, and science, so they are eliminated. But these courses are the ones where students learn how to be creative and solve problems. These courses should remain in the curriculum because they are the ones that allow students to test out their ideas and learn through direct experience how to become proficient at certain skills.

Problem solving, responsibility, time management, collaboration, and communication, on the other hand, are life skills that should be taught in all subjects. Some subjects lend themselves to learning technical skills, but life skills may be learned in all subjects. Educators need to incorporate life skill development in all subjects, and it is possible to do this using many of the current state content standards.

The problem, however, is that most states have created hundreds of standards and benchmarks that students must learn before they graduate. The state of Minnesota's Academic High School Standards (grades 9–12), for example, include hundreds of benchmarks that students are supposed to learn by the time they graduate. The science standards alone include 148 benchmarks. Box 4.1 presents the first page from the science section of the Minnesota Academic Standards for grades 9 through 12 (Minnesota Department of Education, 2009). In order to cover all these benchmarks, teachers must gloss over textbook information and move to the next benchmark. There are not enough days in the school year to adequately cover all these standards and benchmarks. Trying to cover all this content is a nightmare for teachers.

Content benchmarks need to be revised. Policy makers need to eliminate some of them so that teachers can adequately cover them, and they need to revise the wording so that they include action verbs that allow students to practice these skills. Some of the current benchmarks for the state of Minnesota use action verbs such as *use*, *describe*, and *demonstrate*, which suggest that students are allowed to practice skills such as public speaking and communication by actually using, describing, and demonstrating their knowledge.

I wonder, though, how often this actually happens in the classroom. I applaud educators who are allowing students to demonstrate their knowl-

---

Box 4.1.   Benchmarks, Grades 9–12

Strand 1: The Nature of Science and Engineering
Standard 1: Science is a way of knowing about the natural world and is character-ized by empirical criteria, logical argument, and skeptical review.

Benchmarks:

1. Explain the implications of the assumption that the rules of the universe are the same everywhere and these rules can be discovered by careful and systematic investigation.
2. Understand that scientists conduct investigations for a variety of reasons, including: to discover new aspects of the natural world, to explain observed phenomena, to test the conclusions of prior investigations, or to test the predic-tions of current theories.
3. Explain how the traditions and norms of science define the bounds of profes-sional scientific practice and reveal instances of scientific error or misconduct.
    For example: The use of peer review, publications and presentations.
4. Explain how societal and scientific ethics impact research practices.
    For example: Research involving human subjects may be conducted only with the informed consent of the subjects.
5. Identify sources of bias and explain how bias might influence the direction of research and the interpretation of data.
    For example: How funding of research can influence questions studied, pro-cedures used, analysis of data, and communication of results.
6. Describe how changes in scientific knowledge generally occur in incremental steps that include and build on earlier knowledge.
7. Explain how scientific and technological innovations—as well as new evi-dence—can challenge portions of, or entire accepted theories and models including, but not limited to: cell theory, atomic theory, theory of evolution, plate tectonic theory, germ theory of disease, and the big bang theory.

---

edge by explaining or showing what they know, but the problem with these state standards and benchmarks is that they focus on having students memorize dates and facts. The way in which students demonstrate their knowledge in traditional classrooms is to have them take multiple-choice tests. State policy makers should minimize the number of content bench-marks and think of them as skills for students to learn.

In addition to the state content standards, another set of standards, called the National Core Standards, has been developed by the Council of Chief State School Officers (CCSSO) and the National Governors Association (NGA) with the intention of having all fifty states adopt them. One set of National Standards is for English language arts and literacy in history/social studies, science, and technical subjects, and a second set was developed for math. So far forty-one states have adopted these National Standards.

The CCSSO and NGA developed these standards based on research about college and career readiness (CCR) on what students need to learn in order to equip themselves for the challenges of attending college or beginning a career. "As specified by CCSSO and NGA, the Standards are (1) research and evidence based, (2) aligned with college and work expectations, (3) rigorous, and (4) internationally benchmarked" (Common Core State Standards for English Language Arts and Literacy in History/ Social Studies, Science, and Technical Subjects, 2010, p. 3).

The National Core Standards are different from content standards. States developed their own standards and benchmarks based on what content they believed students should learn for each subject area, whereas the National Core Standards refer specifically to literacy in the different content areas. One will notice when reading the National Core Standards that they use similar words for all the standards in each subject area, such as *cite*, *explain*, and *analyze*. Here is some introductory information stated under the section on standards for literacy in history/social studies, science, and technical subjects in the National Core Standards:

> Reading is critical to building knowledge in history/social studies as well as in science and technical subjects. College and career ready reading in these fields requires an appreciation of the norms and conventions of each discipline, such as the kinds of evidence used in history and science; an understanding of domain-specific words and phrases; an attention to precise details; and the capacity to evaluate intricate arguments, synthesize complex information, and follow detailed descriptions of events and concepts in history/social studies. (Common Core State Standards for English Language Arts and Literacy in History/Social Studies, Science, and Technical Subjects, 2010, p. 59)

These standards imply that students should be able to read, comprehend, and analyze the material. Reading, comprehension, and analysis are basic skills that should be interwoven in all subjects all the time. Educators should be doing this all the time with their students.

On one hand, this raises a question as to whether educators really need another set of standards that explain the importance of teaching students reading, comprehension, and analysis. Policy makers have created yet another set of standards that are above and beyond the state content standards, and I fear that more standardized tests will be developed to determine whether students have met these National Standards.

On the other hand, these standards state that students should not only be able to read, comprehend, and analyze the information, but they should also be able to demonstrate their knowledge.

> The grades 6–12 standards on the following pages define what students should understand and be able to do by the end of each grade span. They correspond to the College and Career Readiness (CCR) anchor standards below by number. The CCR and grade-specific standards are necessary complements—the former providing broad standards, the latter providing additional specificity—that together define the skills and understandings that all students must demonstrate. (Common Core State Standards for English Language Arts and Literacy in History/Social Studies, Science, and Technical Subjects, 2010, p. 59)

The operative word in this quote is *demonstrate*. However, how this word is interpreted by policy makers and educators is critical. I wonder if the word *demonstrate* will be interpreted to mean creating more bubble tests to demonstrate knowledge.

Educators have a difficult enough time covering all the benchmarks in the state standards, let alone trying to cover the new National Standards as well. One solution to this problem is to adopt the National Core Standards and focus learning outcomes on demonstration, which should be interpreted as allowing students to show or tell teachers what they know and use performance-based assessments as the way to measure student achievement.

Educators need fewer rather than more standards because more standards will increase the problem of breadth over depth. Standards are important, but fewer standards will allow educators to go into more depth, which will result in a deeper level of learning. Having students demonstrate their knowledge through presentations, for example, will allow students to practice and learn important life skills.

Adopting the National Standards and minimizing the number of state content benchmarks will allow educators to focus on depth of material. Obviously content will be covered, but the National Core Standards, if implemented properly, will allow educators to focus the students' learning on demonstration of the content they are learning. The timing is perfect to begin aligning teaching strategies with the new National Core Standards. This is how it can be accomplished.

Here are the standards for reading for literacy in history/social studies in the National Core Standards for grades 11 to 12:

Key Ideas and Details

1. Cite specific textual evidence to support analysis of primary and secondary sources, connecting insights gained from specific details to an understanding of the text as a whole.
2. Determine the central ideas or information of a primary or secondary source; provide an accurate summary that makes clear the relationships among the key details and ideas.
3. Evaluate various explanations for actions or events and determine which explanation best accords with textual evidence, acknowledging where the text leaves matters uncertain.

Craft and Structure

4. Determine the meaning of words and phrases as they are used in a text, including analyzing how an author uses and refines the meaning of a key term over the course of a text (e.g., how Madison defines faction in Federalist No. 10).
5. Analyze in detail how a complex primary source is structured, including how key sentences, paragraphs, and larger portions of the text contribute to the whole.
6. Evaluate authors' differing points of view on the same historical event or issue by assessing the authors' claims, reasoning, and evidence.

Integration of Ideas and Knowledge

7. Integrate and evaluate multiple sources of information presented in diverse formats and media (e.g., visually, quantitatively, as well as in words) in order to address a question or solve a problem.

8. Evaluate an author's premises, claims, and evidence by corroborating or challenging them with other information.
9. Integrate information from diverse sources, both primary and secondary, into a coherent understanding of an idea or event, noting discrepancies among sources. (Common Core State Standards for English Language Arts and Literacy in History/Social Studies, Science, and Technical Subjects, 2010, p. 61)

In order for students to learn these standards they must be allowed to evaluate, analyze, and integrate the information by doing something with it other than filling in circles on a multiple-choice test. For example, students could create a poster of the major battles in Vietnam and then interview someone such as a parent, relative, or family friend who was in a war and include this information on the poster. Students could present their posters to classmates and explain the significance of the battles, as well as how war impacted the person they interviewed. This will not only allow them to explain the battles but will also personalize the learning by explaining how it impacted the person they interviewed. Having students create products, which are followed by presentations, will allow them to cite information, determine the meaning of words, analyze the information, and integrate it by explaining the meaning of it and how it relates to them.

PERFORMANCE-BASED ASSESSMENT

According to the Met Life Survey of the American Teacher that surveyed 1,000 teachers, 2,002 students, 12,580 parents, and 301 business executives from Fortune 1000 companies, "The critical components of being college- and career-ready focus more on higher-order thinking and performance skills than knowledge of challenging content. Problem-solving skills, critical thinking, the ability to write clearly and persuasively and the ability to work independently—nine in ten of each of the key stakeholders in middle and high school education believe these four skills and abilities are absolutely essential or very important for a student to be ready for college and a career" (2010, p. 12).

This survey suggests that the current assessment system must change to keep pace with education so that educators can use strategies and techniques that allow students to practice critical thinking and demonstrate knowledge by practicing life skills. If teachers could teach their content but focus on students' performance rather than on students' ability to memorize the content, teachers could begin developing meaningful relationships and have more authentic discussions with students.

K–12 education, and many faculty in higher education, have put all of their eggs in one basket. Educators are teaching content for the sake of remembering content. The content is being used as an end in itself, where it should be used as a means to a greater end—skill development. Educators should be using the content to help students learn necessary life skills.

If education changed to a performance-based assessment system, classrooms would look very different than they do now. Students would be actively engaged using technology to create products in the classroom. They would be creating things with their hands, presenting information verbally to their teachers and peers, showing their teachers and peers what they created, and explaining what they learned during the process.

According to Stiggins, Arter, Chappuis, and Chappuis, performance-based assessments are when "students engage in an activity that requires them to apply a performance skill or create a product and we judge its quality" (2006, p. 191). Educators can observe students performing skills when they do presentations or work in small groups, and products are things like proposals, outlines, plans, blueprints, drafts, models, videos, papers, biographies, portfolios, and websites (Markham, Larmer, and Ravitz, 2003).

Every day the classroom focus would be on providing students opportunities to demonstrate what they are learning, and students would not only be learning the course content, but they would also be practicing skills like time management, responsibility, decision making, and problem solving. Students would come to class, and rather than the teacher doing all the talking, they would be engaged in activities such as using new forms of technology, working on projects, solving problems, working in groups, and presenting their ideas to classmates.

In this new system, educators would focus on observing students performing skills by using the content in their specific subject areas. The evaluation process would include different assessment tools such as rubrics and portfolios, and knowledge and skills could be evaluated multiple times during the school year to determine student growth.

The current assessment system uses standardized tests consisting primarily of multiple-choice questions. Below is a sample of questions from an Advanced Placement history test taken from the College Board website. Multiple-choice test questions like these are the norm and are used in most subjects.

By the end of the seventeenth century, which of the following was true of women in New England?

(a) They had begun to challenge their subordinate role in society.
(b) They were a majority in many church congregations.
(c) They voted in local elections.
(d) They frequently divorced their husbands.
(e) They could lead town meetings.

The First Great Awakening led to all of the following EXCEPT

(a) separatism and secession from established churches
(b) the renewed persecution of witches
(c) the growth of institutions of higher learning
(d) a flourishing of the missionary spirit
(e) a greater appreciation for the emotional experiences of faith

The Embargo Act of 1807 had which of the following effects on the United States?

(a) It severely damaged American manufacturing.
(b) It enriched many cotton plantation owners.
(c) It disrupted American shipping.
(d) It was ruinous to subsistence farmers.
(e) It had little economic impact.

The idea of Manifest Destiny included all of the following beliefs EXCEPT:

(a) Commerce and industry would decline as the nation expanded its agricultural base.
(b) The use of land for settled agriculture was preferable to its use for nomadic hunting.
(c) Westward expansion was both inevitable and beneficial.
(d) God had selected America as a chosen land and people.
(e) The ultimate extent of the American domain was to be from the tropics to the Arctic.

Knowing the answers to these questions requires students to read the information and recite it in their heads until it sticks. The only skill students are practicing while preparing for this kind of test is rote memorization.

Another way to approach this material would be to have students use technology to do projects on these topics and teach each other this information through presentations. For example, students could break into small groups and gather information about women's role in the seventeenth century, the Great Awakening, the Embargo Act, and Manifest Destiny and create a poster board, PowerPoint presentation, video, or some combination of the three. They could collect detailed information about how these topics changed the United States and how they impacted the thinking during that time, and then provide a presentation to the class.

The assessment process would look very different from a multiple-choice test and could focus on life skills. Table 4.1 is an example of a rubric that could be used to assess life skills students are learning while doing these projects.

Projects are an excellent way to assess life skills because students have to use technology, create a product, solve problems throughout the process of creating a product, communicate with their team members, be responsible for doing their portion of the project, make group decisions, and learn to collaborate as they work together to complete it. When students are doing projects they are learning more than just the academic content. They are learning how to collaborate and how to be self-directed learners. Students are still learning content, but they would be evaluated on their ability to demonstrate their knowledge of it as opposed to memorizing it.

Rubrics could be used to assess the project process; however, other rubrics could be used to assess students' oral presentations of these projects. Table 4.2 is an example of an oral rubric taken from the Technology Applications Center for Educator Development website.

Using assessment tools like these could become rather time consuming, especially if educators decided to create a separate rubric for each life skill. However, if the current assessment system was altered and focused on learning life skills, then teachers could turn their attention to creating different assessment tools and spend less time preparing students for state-mandated tests.

In a conversation I had with a teacher/advisor from Minnesota New Country School in Henderson, Minnesota, he talked about how the project

Table 4.1.   Life Skills Rubric

	Novice	Proficient	Advanced
Creativity	Project shows little originality.	Project has some unique features.	Project is original and unique from the others.
Problem Solving with poster board, PowerPoint, and/or video.	Little or no problem solving was involved. Students accepted first option available.	Students learned how to use two of the three options.	Students learned how to use all three options in their project.
Decision Making	Consensus process was used 25% or less of the time.	Consensus was used 50% or less of the time.	Consensus was used 90% or more of the time
Time Management	Students made efficient use of time 25% or less.	Students made efficient use of time 50% of the time.	Students made efficient use of time 90% or more of the time.
Finding Information	Students did not research all options available. Chose first resource to create project.	Students used adequate number of resources to find information.	Students used multiple resources to find necessary information.
Responsibility	Student was responsible 25% or less of the time for collecting data.	Student was responsible 50% or more of the time for collecting data.	Student was responsible 90% or more of the time for collecting data.
Team Player	Students worked together in a collaborative fashion 25% or less of the time.	Students worked together in a collaborative fashion 50% or more of the time.	Students worked together in a collaborative fashion 90% or more of the time.

process changes the students' way of thinking. Students move away from believing they have to memorize information, becoming self-directed learners who realize they are in charge of their own learning.

They realize through this process that they are responsible for creating useful projects, managing their time, communicating with their advisor and peers, following through with their learning commitments, and

Table 4.2.   Oral Presentation Rubric

Criteria	0	1	2	3
Nonverbal Skills				
Eye Contact	Does not attempt to look at audience at all, reads notes the entire time.	Only focuses attention to one particular part of the class, does not scan audience.	Occasionally looks at someone or some groups during presentation.	Constantly looks at someone or some groups at all times.
Facial Expressions	Has either a deadpan expression or shows a conflicting expression during entire presentation.	Occasionally displays both a deadpan and conflicting expression during presentation.	Occasionally demonstrates either a deadpan or conflicting expression during presentation.	Gives audience clues to what the content of speech is about; appropriate expression, never notice a deadpan or conflicting expression.
Gestures	No gestures are noticed.			Natural hand gestures are demonstrated.
Posture	Sits during presentation or slumps.		Occasionally slumps during presentation.	Stands up straight with both feet on the ground.
Vocal Skills				
Enthusiasm	Shows absolutely no interest in topic presented.	Shows some negativity toward topic presented.	Occasionally shows positive feelings about topic.	Demonstrates a strong positive feeling about topic during entire presentation.
Vocalized Pauses (uh, well uh, um)	10 or more are noticed.	6–9 are noticed.	1–5 are noticed.	No vocalized pauses noticed.

Content

Topic Announced	Audience has no idea what the report is on.		Vaguely tells audience what report is over.	Clearly explains what the report is covering.
Time Frame	Presentation is less than minimum time.	Presentation is more than maximum time.		Presentation falls within required time frame.
Visual Aid	Poor, distracts audience and is hard to read.	Adds nothing to presentation.	Thoughts articulated clearly, but not engaging.	Visual aid enhances presentation, all thoughts articulated and keeps interest.
Completeness of Content	One or more points left out.	Majority of points glossed over.	Majority of points covered in depth, some points glossed over.	Thoroughly explains all points.
Professionalism of Presentation	Mumbles, audience has difficulty hearing, confusing.	Thoughts don't flow, not clear, does not engage audience.	Thoughts articulated clearly, though does not engage audience.	Presentation is organized, and the interest level of the audience is maintained.

developing coherent presentations that will be evaluated by advisors, peers, community members, and parents. Rubrics are used for evaluating students, but the discussion that follows the student's presentation determines whether the student has completed the project satisfactorily, or whether the student will need to continue working on the project to meet the expectations of his or her advisory committee.

Educators can use rubrics to evaluate students; however, students could use similar rubrics to evaluate each other, and themselves. Rubrics like these would allow educators to focus more on formative rather than summative assessments, and the goal would be to have these skills improve over time.

Much of our education system focuses on summative assessments. For example, in a biology class the teacher covers unit one in the textbook, which might be on cell formation. Students are tested on this information and the teacher proceeds to unit two, which might be on photosynthesis, and the students are then tested again at the end of this unit. This process continues throughout the quarter or semester. Little time, if any, is spent on connecting the information from one unit to the others; therefore learning becomes compartmentalized and disconnected.

This is a summative assessment process because students are tested periodically throughout the quarter or semester on each unit, which covers different content. Students are not given a chance to be tested as many times as needed to get all the questions correct. Instead, the teacher moves on to a new unit with new content, and students are tested again at the end of the unit.

According to Popham (2008, p. 24), formative assessments focus on improving knowledge and skills over time: "The target curricular aim is typically a skill (rather than a body of knowledge) and usually a significant skill at that—the kind of learning outcome requiring a number of lessons for students to achieve it."

For example, students could be assessed on life skills such as problem solving, time management, and responsibility after unit one, and then assessed again on these same skills after unit two to see if they have improved over time. The goal is to have these skills improve during the quarter or semester.

Formative assessments change the mind-set of the teacher and student. The goal is not to memorize information; instead it is to demonstrate knowledge and practice life skills. With formative assessments, educators could evaluate students, but students could also evaluate themselves periodically and then compare their results with the teacher's assessment.

With formative performance-based assessments, teachers could explain to students what they can do differently to improve upon their skills. This process requires communication with students and requires teachers to create more personal relationships with students.

The current system has dehumanized education. Educators do not have time to develop relationships with their students because they are too busy following all the rules and regulations to meet AYP. Once again, this is not the educators' fault. They need to prepare students for tests, which requires time to cover all the necessary benchmarks and making sure students know what will be on the tests. The testing bureaucracy is preventing them from getting to know their students. Students feel disconnected from their teachers and often feel that their teachers do not have time to help them when they do not understand the material.

In this new system, educators would have to spend more time communicating with their students about their projects and presentations. Content would become secondary, and the skills would become primary. However, as mentioned before, students are still learning content because they have to demonstrate their knowledge of it. The difference is that they are exploring a topic on a deeper level, which allows for more depth but less breadth.

Performance-based assessments take students to a deeper level of understanding. Not only do they need to know facts, but they also need to be able to explain the information to their class. Knowing the correct answer is not enough; they need to understand the information well enough to express their ideas on the significance and meaning of the information. During this process students are learning how to work together with others, research information, and create coherent presentations.

Educators need to change their focus and emphasize depth over breadth. Information continues to grow at an astronomical rate. Textbooks become thicker every year as new information is discovered. Eventually there will not be enough time to cover all the information in a book. In fact, most educators I talk to say there is not enough time now for them to cover all the material! Going deeper into a topic allows them to not only learn information, but it also allows them to practice necessary life skills.

If performance-based evaluations replaced state-mandated standardized tests, then memorization would no longer be the most dominant learning process, and direct instruction would no longer be the preferred teaching method. Direct instruction would become less used because students would no longer need to memorize information contained in each benchmark. Performance evaluations should become the more common way to assess student learning, and AYP should be based on performing skills rather than on memorizing information.

Keep in mind that a performance-based assessment system is the catalyst to changing the learning process, but the assessment is not the most important piece of this equation. Learning life skills is what matters most, and to learn these skills students must be allowed to practice them.

PRODUCTS

One way to assess student performance is by having students create products like proposals, outlines, videos, and papers. Benchmarks can be easily applied to products because students must evaluate, analyze, and integrate knowledge when they are creating them. Products can be created individually or in small groups. The product itself can be assessed for quality, but educators can also observe and assess students' life skill development when they are working on products. Markham et al. (2003) created a list of different types of products that students can create, which I adapted for this book (see table 4.3).

Creating products requires students to do research, gather information, take measurements, draw designs, input data, work with tools, and engage in hands-on learning. Students can learn technical and life skills while they are involved in creating products. Different types of products focus on different technical skills. For example, written ones focus on learning writing skills, whereas computer technology products focus on learning how to use different software programs.

They can also help students learn life skills. For example, creating any of the products mentioned requires students to learn time-management, organization, responsibility, decision-making, and self-directed learning

Table 4.3. Types of Products

Written Products	Computer Technology	Media Products	Planning Products	Construction Products
Research report	Web designs	Drawings	Proposals	Physical models
Papers	Videos	Paintings	Estimates	Consumer products
Letters	Podcasts	Collages	Bids	Machines
Posters	Computer programs	Maps	Blueprints	Woodwork
Proposals	PowerPoints	Scrapbooks	CAD drawings	Metalwork
Poems	Databases	Photo albums	Flowcharts	Sculptures
Brochures	Graphics		Tables	Pottery
Surveys	CD-ROM		Graphs	
Essays			Timelines	
Book reviews				
Movie scripts				

skills. When students are given a task to create a product, and then given the freedom to create it, they must practice these life skills.

Students can be evaluated in two ways with products. The quality of the product itself can be evaluated, and observing the life skills they are learning through the process of creating the product can also be evaluated. Specific criteria can be created for both the quality of the product and for the life skills they should be learning during the process.

Rubrics can be developed that include specific criteria for quality and life skill development. Table 4.4 is a podcast rubric created by Jose Garcia for his seventh-grade science class. This is an excellent example of how a rubric can include the quality of the product, life skill development, and technical skill development. The first two categories, of "Research" and "Copyright Laws," focus on the quality of the podcast, the fourth category titled "Podcast," focuses on technical computer skills, and the fifth and sixth categories focus on life skill development that includes collaboration and organization.

Observing students working on their products helps educators evaluate students' life skill development. Students tend to have less-developed life skills, especially when they are new to creating products, but as time goes by and they create more products, they learn how to improve these skills.

Many educators already have students create these types of products but evaluate only the product itself. It is important to evaluate the quality of the product, but it is also important to evaluate life skills at the same time. Combining both quality and life skills on rubrics adds strength to

Table 4.4.   Rubric

Category	4	3	2	1
Research	Student researched topic and integrated **5 or more quality** pieces of information into podcast.	Student researched topic and integrated **4 quality** pieces of information into podcast.	Student researched topic and integrated **3 quality** pieces of information into podcast.	Student researched topic and integrated less than **2 quality** pieces of information into podcast.
Copyright Laws	Copyright laws followed at all times. **No errors.**	Copyright laws followed most of the time. **1–2 errors found.**	Copyright laws violated frequently. **3–4 errors found.**	Copyright laws disregarded or missing.
Point of View–Purpose	Podcast establishes a purpose and maintains that focus throughout. **No errors.**	Podcast establishes a purpose at the beginning, but **wanders 1–2 times** from topic focus.	Podcast purpose is somewhat clear, but many aspects of the podcast seem only slightly related. **Wanders 3–4 times** from topic focus.	It was difficult to figure out the purpose of the podcast. **Wanders 5 or more** times from topic focus.
Podcast	Podcast supports overall project. Student has a good grasp of the specified project process, using the technology to its fullest potential. **No errors.**	Podcast lacks project support. Student has a good grasp of the specified project process; could have better used the technology. **1–2 errors.**	Podcast does not support project. Student has an adequate grasp of the specified project process. Technology was not used accurately. **3–4 errors.**	Podcast is missing or completely disorganized. Student seems not to understand the specified project process. **5 or more errors.**

Student Participation	Student listened to, shared with, and supported the efforts of others. Student was always on task! **No errors.**	Student functioned fairly well. Listened to, shared with, and supported the efforts of others. Student was almost always on task! **1–2 times corrected.**	Student functioned well. Student was often off task! **3–4 times corrected.**	Student was often off task and/or was overtly disrespectful to others in the team. **5 times or more corrected.**
Thinking Map	Thinking Map summarizes overall project. Thinking Map is well organized and contains frame of reference. **No errors.**	Thinking Map summary lacks project support. Thinking Map is relatively organized and contains frame of reference. **1–2 errors.**	Thinking Map does not summarize project clearly. Thinking Map is disorganized and lacks frame of reference. **3–4 errors.**	Thinking Map is missing or completely disorganized. **5 errors or more.**

Student Name:	(4+4+4+4+4)	Attendance	Final Grade
Teacher Comments:			
Student Name:	(4+4+4+4+4)	**Attendance**	**Final Grade**
Teacher Comments:			
Student Name:	(4+4+4+4+4)	**Attendance**	**Final Grade**
Teacher Comments:			

the assessment process. They are both important and can provide students with information on how to improve upon their skill development.

PRESENTATIONS

Products should be followed by presentations, which will allow students to discuss ideas and present them to teachers and peers. Having students do presentations provides them with opportunities to evaluate, analyze, and integrate knowledge, as well as to demonstrate their knowledge.

The ideal learning environment while teaching these standards is to use one of the teaching approaches mentioned in chapter 3 combined with student presentations. Sometimes, however, educators are not able to use these teaching approaches due to time constraints, but student presentations can be easily implemented at the end of lesson units. Students can do short presentations of three to five minutes, which allows them to learn how to organize their thoughts and express their ideas.

Presentations are one of the better ways to assess students' knowledge because they can't fake it. They have to understand the information well enough to explain it to their peers and teachers, and it is easy to determine if students don't understand the material. Presentations are critical in helping students not only to develop life skills, but also to help them learn to appreciate the skills they are learning.

Jere Brophy, who teaches in Michigan State University's Department of Education, suggests that, "If a curriculum strand has significant value for learners, it will be because its content network is structured around big ideas that provide a basis for authentic applications to life outside of school" (2008, p. 135). Presentations will allow students to take the curriculum strands, which often start with the big idea, and apply meaning to them.

Brophy suggests there are three things educators can do to help students appreciate what they are learning:

1. Make wise choices about what content and learning activities to include, to ensure that what the students are asked to learn is worth learning.
2. Introduce lessons in ways that include explaining the value and modeling applications of the big ideas or skills to be developed.

3. Engage students in activities that afford opportunities for them to develop and apply this content in ways that enable them to discover its value through firsthand experience with it, and scaffold their engagement so as to help them to notice and appreciate the activities' empowering affordances. (2008, p. 138)

Presentations allow students to learn skills like time management, public speaking, and organization, and they also provide firsthand experience when students cite, analyze, and explain what they learned while creating their presentations. Presentations are critical to the learning process, but they also provide educators with an opportunity to accurately assess what students have learned from these experiences.

Educators do not use presentations often enough because of time constraints, but this is where much of the important learning occurs. This process allows students to learn how to present their ideas in a logical order and allows them to express their ideas and apply what they are learning because they must explain to their classmates and teachers what they learned from reading the texts.

Students teaching students should be used more often because it works. According to Muir and van der Linden (2009), students enjoy doing presentations and gain a deeper understanding of the content by doing them. Their research focused on undergraduate psychology students who taught psychological concepts to elementary school children. In their study they surveyed approximately 515 students and found that 97 percent agreed it was a valuable experience, 98 percent agreed it was an enjoyable experience, 89 percent agreed that they increased their knowledge of psychology, and 90 percent agreed that presentations should be a regular part of the course (2009, p. 171). When students enjoy their learning and feel that it has value, they will be more motivated to learn.

Certain charter schools across North America rely heavily on presentations as a tool to evaluate student learning. Littky and Grabelle (2004), intricately involved with the Metropolitan Regional Career and Technical Center (MET) school, describe presentations as "kids getting up and talking passionately about a book they've read, a paper they've written, drawings they've made, or even what they know about auto mechanics. It is a way for students to have conversations about the things they have learned" (p. 7).

Project-based charter schools such as the ones created by EdVisions also have their students do presentations after completing their projects. They hold presentations routinely where the public is invited to listen to students present on their projects. They also have students do a major presentation after completing their senior projects, which usually require three hundred to four hundred hours of research. When students do presentations, they "take their projects more seriously, they get valuable practice speaking in public, the parents better understand the learning process, the public knows the school is serious about academics, and it builds community" (Newell, 2005, p. 14).

College students also enjoy presentations because they are opportunities to teach their peers about their own personal experiences with different strategies, techniques, and applications that they have experimented with in their own learning environments. I asked my graduate students why they like doing presentations, and here are some of their responses (Experiential Learning and Education Reform Course, personal communication, April 13, 2011):

It challenges me to organize and refine my thoughts.
It provides for a democratic environment where all voices are heard.
It boosts my self-confidence when I express my ideas in front of my peers.
It allows me to think critically about views that I don't agree with.
It allows me to practice and develop stronger speaking skills.
It allows me to articulate my position on ideas.

Having students present their work helps solidify their learning and should be required in all high school and college courses.

Presentations help students learn essential skills for the workplace; they learn how to evaluate and analyze information, they learn how to organize their thoughts, they learn how to express their ideas and opinions, and they learn how to reflect on the important things they have learned during the process. When presentations are required assignments, it allows students to speak about what they read and turn abstract information into meaningful information. Presentations allow them to comprehend and speak more intelligently about the subject matter because they must test out their ideas and understanding of the material by explaining what they learned in front of peers and teachers.

Newbrey and Baltezore state that research poster presentations are being used more often in high school and college courses because they help students "improve written, visual, and verbal communication skills" (2006, p. 550). Poster presentations use an inquiry-based approach to learning because students must do research on their topics and explore key concepts that they will include on their posters. Students learn to be creative and use their artistic side when designing posters because they must use pictures, graphs, tables, and background colors that are aesthetically appealing to their audience.

Educators can identify the specifications of the poster, which might include overall size, background, layout, and content. Students need some structure when creating posters, but too much structure might inhibit students' creativity. Typically, posters include title and author information, body of the text, graphs and tables, and pictures.

Posters provide the visual for the audience, but the other important aspect is the presentation itself. Students must understand the material and be able to articulate the information contained on the poster. This is where students learn how to organize their thoughts and to accurately express the ideas and information on the poster. Once again, time frame is important to consider as some classroom educators may not be able to afford giving up several class periods in order for students to do presentations, but short ones are better than none at all.

Chapter Five

Preparing Educators for
New School Models

While visiting a local project-based-learning charter school I was introduced to a young woman who was doing her student teaching to fulfill her requirements for a master of arts in teaching. I asked her what she had learned in her undergraduate and graduate programs that prepared her to do her student teaching at this school and she raised her hand and formed a zero. It struck me at that moment that many teacher education programs are not preparing future educators to teach in schools that focus on project-based or other experiential approaches to learning.

According to Rubenstein (2007, p. 1), "Far too many of America's 1,200-plus schools of education are mired in methods that isolate education from the arts and sciences, segregate the theory and practice of teaching, and provide insufficient time and support for future teachers to learn to work in real classrooms." In order for teacher candidates to learn how to teach at innovative schools, they must be exposed to new teaching approaches being used at these schools and be provided with opportunities to observe and teach in these schools.

When I ask educators questions such as, what motivates you to learn, how do you learn best, and what engages you most in your learning, their answers are fairly similar. They are motivated to learn when they are engaged in activities and are learning skills that are meaningful and relevant to their lives. They learn best by doing things, not just by reading or discussing things. They are more engaged when they are immersed in experiences that are often outside the classroom and entail working with other people toward a common goal. Finally, they are most engaged when they are allowed the freedom to learn what is most relevant to them.

Their responses indicate that they enjoy learning when they are actively involved in the learning process.

A new assessment model focusing on hands-on learning for teacher candidates that is being used at California State University, Fullerton (Teaching Performance Assessment, n.d.), is called the Teaching Performance Assessment (TPA). The TPA model includes these four tasks:

1. Subject-Specific Pedagogy Task
2. Designing Instruction Task
3. Assessing Learning Task
4. Culminating Teaching Experience Task

The first three tasks are completed with real students with whom teacher candidates are working in their schools. The last task involves videotaping the teacher candidate with real students in the classroom, and provides candidates with feedback on ways to improve their teaching. This model provides candidates with hands-on practical learning in real-world settings and is based on repeated assessments of their teaching performance. Educators believe performance assessments are more effective for them than paper-and-pencil tests. If they are correct, then why shouldn't educators use this same type of assessment to evaluate their students' progress?

High school students are no different from educators in how they like to learn. "Students are most excited and engaged by teaching methods in which they learn with their peers; students are also engaged by activities in which they are active participants; students are least engaged in activities in which they do not play an active role" (Yazzie-Mintz, 2006, p. 7). If this is how students like to learn, as well as educators, then why aren't teacher education programs preparing their teacher candidates to use more hands-on learning in their classrooms and to evaluate students based on their performance?

Educators are responsible for providing students with learning that is exciting and meaningful; they are older, they have more education, and they have more life experience, but in order for them to motivate and engage their students they must be exposed to new school models and be educated on how to use innovative approaches to teaching. Teacher education programs must incorporate these new approaches and assessments in their curriculums.

I have had numerous teachers take my experiential education courses at the university where I work, and at the end of these courses many of them come to me and say something similar to this: "I believe in the philosophy of experiential learning, and I know that it works better than using lectures and tests, but it is not practical." Under the current assessment system, educators find it difficult to use experiential learning techniques because it takes more time to implement them, and these techniques are not as efficient at getting students the information they need for the tests. Teachers are being held accountable for their students' test scores, when they should be held accountable for their students' ability to apply their learning. Teacher candidates must be exposed to other types of approaches besides just direct instruction.

It appears that many teacher preparation programs focus their curriculums on teaching in traditional public education settings; however, there are numerous schools cropping up around the country that use innovative approaches to teaching that help students learn life skills. These schools do not emphasize memorization and test taking like many traditional public schools; instead they believe that the process of learning should be relevant to students, include authentic experiences, and require students to solve problems while learning to think critically.

These schools focus their attention on engaging students in their learning by using experiential learning techniques such as projects, activities, and field experiences. An important objective is to inspire and motivate students to learn, and these schools understand that experiential learning is the way to do this. Experiential learning is not something that teacher preparation programs spend much time on because they focus their attention on theories and techniques that attempt to raise test scores and close the achievement gap.

Students are learning content in these new schools, but they are also learning how to become self-directed learners. Students are allowed some freedom to determine the types of projects, activities, and field experiences they wish to engage in, and the teachers act more like guides helping them move forward in the learning process as they engage in activities, create projects, and undergo field experiences. Unfortunately, teacher preparation programs are not exposing candidates to these new models, so these new schools must train teachers to teach at their schools.

In the next section of this chapter I have identified six organizations that are promoting innovative models of schooling: EdVisions Inc., Big Picture Learning, Expeditionary Learning, High Tech High, New Tech High, and Gateway to College National Network (GtCNN). I chose these organizations because they all rely heavily on experiential learning, they all realize the importance of teaching life skills, they all have conducted research that proves their teaching approaches inspire and motivate students to do well, and they have all received significant grants from various foundations.

These organizations use experiential learning as the centerpiece of their curriculums, and all of them except Gateway to College National Network help K–12 schools convert themselves to specific design principles created by these organizations. Schools must meet some or all of their design principles in order to brand themselves as one of these schools.

GtCNN is different from the others in that they offer postsecondary programs that help students transition into college. GtCNN offers start-up assistance directly to communities and colleges that partner with multiple school districts in their service area. Their programs are housed in community colleges, and they provide students with project-based learning activities with the intention of helping them succeed in college.

A brief overview of each organization is provided, with specific attention given to the teaching and learning philosophy of each. The overview is followed by an interview with a key stakeholder of the organization. Key stakeholders from the K–12 organizations were asked the following two questions.

1. How do you think teacher preparation programs should be training teachers to teach in your schools?
2. What does your organization do to prepare teachers to teach in your schools?

The above two questions were slightly modified for the GtCNN stakeholder because their focus is on transitioning students into higher education and training college instructors to use effective instructional strategies, including project-based learning.

INNOVATIVE SCHOOL MODELS

EdVisions' Schools

In 2001 the Bill and Melinda Gates Foundation awarded a grant to Ed-Visions for the purpose of replicating the project-based learning (PBL) model that was used at Minnesota New Country School (MNCS) in Henderson, Minnesota. Since 2001, EdVisions Inc. has helped create over forty-five schools across the United States modeled after their design essentials.

EdVisions Inc. "design essentials" are characterized by four main themes: (1) a self-directed, project-based learning program; (2) a student-centered democratic culture; (3) the use of authentic assessment; and (4) teacher ownership and accountability (Newell & Van Ryzin, 2007, p. 468). Student-initiated projects are the centerpiece of EdVisions' schools. Students create and design their own projects with the help of their advisors, and when the projects are completed, students are given credits that are aligned with the state academic standards.

PBL requires continuous conversation, discussion, and evaluation between advisors and students. Students identify a project they would like to do, fill out a project proposal form, negotiate the details of the project with their advisors and advisory committee, do the project, and present it to their advisory committee consisting of students, advisors, parents, and community members.

How do you think teacher preparation programs should be training teachers to teach in your schools?

Doug Thomas, director of EdVisions Inc., suggested that current teacher preparation programs have to stop teaching to one style of learning. The one style he is referring to is direct instruction, which does not motivate students to learn. Instead, he believes programs should create a portfolio of different school models and expose teacher candidates to all these models.

Teacher candidates who are interested in teaching at one of these schools should be provided opportunities to research the school and attempt to gain an understanding of how the school functions, as well as to learn about the methodologies used at the school. Programs should offer teacher candidates multiple immersion experiences where they go to the schools and spend time observing and helping facilitate student learning when possible before they do their student teaching. This way candidates will have a grasp of a variety of school models and will be better equipped to make an informed decision on where they would like to do their student teaching. The outcome that teacher preparation programs should strive for is to match candidates with schools where the experience will be successful for both the candidate and the school.

What does your organization do to prepare teachers to teach in your schools?

Doug mentioned that EdVisions schools offer candidates unlimited opportunities to visit these schools and spend as much time as they like observing students and talking with teachers about methods, policies, and procedures. College students from various departments are allowed to do internships at these schools. Most of the individuals have been from teacher preparation programs; however, there have also been individuals from other university departments who have done internships at these schools.

EdVisions also offers a summer institute that educates individuals on the processes of working for these schools. The summer institute is designed in a way to have participants walk through the processes as if they were a student at the school, which helps them understand how the school operates from a student perspective. EdVisions also offers individual coaches/teachers for individuals wishing to teach at one of these schools. He feels this one-on-one attention is critical in helping individuals who have not been exposed to this model learn about it in a more efficient way (personal communication, May 11, 2011).

Big Picture Learning

In 1995 Dennis Littky and Elliot Washor started Big Picture Learning with the purpose of creating schools that focused on engaging students in their learning by providing them with relevant hands-on experiences in their communities. In 1996 they created the Metropolitan Regional

Career and Technical Center (MET), which has since received considerable notoriety because of its unique approach to educating one student at a time, placing them in the community doing internships and projects that benefit both the student and the partnering organization. Currently there are about 100 Big Picture schools around the world, with 60 located in the United States (personal communication, K. Thierer, June 30, 2011). These schools are based on ten distinguishers, which must all work together in order for students to be successful (Big Picture Learning website, n.d.).

1. Learning in the Real World: LTI
2. One Student at a Time: Personalization
3. Authentic Assessment
4. School Organization
5. Advisory Structure
6. School Culture
7. Leadership
8. Parent/Family Engagement: Adult Support
9. School/College Partnership: College Preparation and Support
10. Professional Development

The heart of the learning process at Big Picture schools is learning through interests/internships, or LTIs. This is where students, through the help of their advisors, identify an interest they would like to pursue, which is generally through an internship. Students then contact a mentor from the organization, determine the specifics of the internship, do the internship, complete one major project while doing the internship, and conduct an exhibition at the end of the internship where students do a formal presentation of what they learned during the internship. Students have a variety of other learning activities they are engaged in during school days; however, internships are a key learning activity at these schools (Littky and Grabelle, 2004).

How do you think teacher preparation programs should be training teachers to teach in your schools?

Elliot Washor, codirector of Big Picture Learning, believes teacher candidates spend way too much time in classroom-based courses that are steeped in theory and lacking in practice. Teacher preparation programs should have their students in classroom settings as much as possible to expose them to the realities of teaching. Teacher candidates need to be in the classroom every day observing and experiencing what they will be doing after they graduate from the program. They need to be immersed in the schools, surrounded by students, teachers, mentors, administrators, and families that are associated with the school where they wish to do their student teaching.

Professors in teacher preparation programs spend too much time discussing theories and techniques that are foreign to the candidates. Candidates will not understand the theories and techniques until they are engaged in the practice of teaching. He suggests that teacher preparation programs should hold classes after the typical school day, and these classes should be used as a mechanism for candidates to discuss and reflect on what they experienced during the school day. Direct experience is key to learning how to teach, and until programs figure this out, candidates will graduate without much experience in knowing how to teach at these innovative schools.

What does your organization do to prepare teachers to teach in your schools?

Big Picture Learning does not have a teacher certification program, although they have had discussions on creating one. They have teacher training programs in the summer, as well as during the school year. They attempt to find individuals who will perform well as teachers in their system, and then educate them to teach according to the Big Picture educational philosophy.

Elliot mentioned that they provide coaches and mentors for new teachers to help them become adjusted to the school. Individuals who have been exposed to using experiential learning models tend to adjust much more quickly to their philosophy than individuals coming from traditional teacher preparation programs. He also mentioned that individuals who have been exposed to service learning with an entrepreneurial flair also seem to adjust much more quickly than others (personal communication, May 23, 2011).

Expeditionary Learning

Although the concepts behind Expeditionary Learning (EL) were initiated in 1987 when the Harvard Outward Bound Project joined forces with the Harvard Graduate School of Education to increase academic rigor with Outward Bound's work in schools, the first expeditionary schools were not created until 1993 when ten schools were selected in five cities: New York, Boston, Denver, Portland, and Dubuque (Expeditionary Learning website, n.d.). These schools were created from a New American Schools Development Corporation $9 million grant. Since that time, Expeditionary Learning has helped create 165 schools all across the country.

Their schools are modeled on five core practices. In order for a school to call itself an Expeditionary Learning school, it must agree to follow and implement all five core practices listed below:

1. Learning Expeditions: Addressing standards through project-based curriculum connecting to real-world need.
2. Active Pedagogy: Infusing dynamic instructional practices that build skills and critical thinking.
3. Culture and Character: Building a schoolwide culture of trust, respect, responsibility, and joy in achievement.
4. Leadership and School Improvement: Strengthening leadership across the school in instruction, culture, and curriculum.
5. Structures: Creating time for student and adult learning, collaboration, and focus on excellence. (Expeditionary Learning website, n.d.)

Learning expeditions are the centerpiece of their curriculum and are created by the teachers. Learning expeditions are usually six to twelve weeks in length and require students to acquire skills in reading, writing, listening, speaking, research, critical thinking, problem solving, and collaboration (Expeditionary Learning, 2011, p. 13). Learning expeditions require students to follow a certain process, which includes formulating guiding questions, selecting case studies, and designing projects and products that include working in the field with experts to do service learning. Service learning in the community is often a culminating experience, which benefits both the community and the students.

For example, students might partner with a local department of natural resources office to test water samples from a local stream to determine how to improve the water quality. This might require students to do presentations at a town hall meeting to discuss their findings and explain ways to reduce stream pollutants. The result might be a service-learning project where students and community members implement a plan to reduce these pollutants. Like some of the other school models mentioned in this section, projects can be small or big, requiring a week or several months to complete.

How do you think teacher preparation programs should be training teachers to teach in your schools?

From Scott Hartl's (president and CEO of Expeditionary Learning) experience working with newly graduated teachers, there are three primary skills that new teachers lack. They know how to give tests and grade tests, but in Expeditionary Learning schools they need knowledge on how to implement formative assessments where they can identify short-term and long-term learning goals and understand how to track student progress while students are attempting to meet their goals. Assessing a learning expedition, which may include completing a semester-long project, requires teachers to broaden their thinking on how and what to assess during this process. A multiple-choice test will provide a summative assessment, but it is much more challenging to assess life skills like critical thinking and responsibility while creating and conducting a project.

A second skill that is lacking is the teacher's ability to creatively apply academic standards to learning expeditions. Teachers must be able to mesh academic standards with learning expeditions because students must meet all academic standards prior to graduating from EL schools. Teachers need to understand the standards and be able to apply them to unique learning experiences at EL schools. Assessing students' knowledge while they are creating a community garden, for example, requires teachers to think about how science or English standards can be met through this experience.

Finally, pedagogical delivery of the standards in EL schools requires teachers to have a thorough understanding of how to engage students in projects that will allow them to apply information over a long period of

time. Teachers need to understand that mastery of skills requires a continuous process where students are allowed, on an ongoing basis, to apply
what they are learning. Teachers need to allow students to go through
numerous trial-and-error attempts in order for students to learn how to
problem solve and think critically.

What does your organization do to prepare teachers to teach
in your schools?

One of the primary functions of EL is professional development for teachers. Teachers wishing to work at an EL school can attend a number of institutes hosted by EL. Last year EL conducted approximately two hundred
institutes that focused on training teachers to teach at EL schools. EL also
provides coaches who will come to a school and mentor teachers on the
EL process (personal communication, May 23, 2011).

High Tech High

High Tech High launched its first charter school in 2000 and currently
operates eleven lottery charter schools in San Diego County. The concept
behind the school was developed by forty high-tech industry leaders who
came together because they were concerned about the lack of individuals,
especially women and minorities, who were qualified to work in the high-
tech industry (High Tech High website, n.d.). The first school, called the
Gary and Jerri-Ann Jacobs High Tech High, was a success, and ten more
schools have since been developed.

High Tech High is unique in that it not only has created multiple charter schools, but it has also created its own teacher credentialing program
and has also started a new graduate school of education complete with
master's degree programs in teacher leadership and school leadership.
Educators can work on their own professional development through these
degree programs while working at a High Tech High school.

There are four design principles that these schools operate under:
personalization, adult world connection, common intellectual mission,
and teacher as designer. The education is personalized because students
design and create projects that are of interest to them, and advisors help
guide them through the learning process. Students do internships and

projects in the community during their junior and senior years, which connects them to adults in the community. There is a common mission to help students develop life skills and prepare them for college and technical education so they can be successful in the work world after graduation. Lastly, teachers work in teams to design and implement interdisciplinary lessons, which helps students connect ideas from one class to the next.

The learning process focuses mostly on project-based learning; however, students have opportunities to do internships out in the community. The PBL process is teacher directed; however, it is always a goal to tap into the interests of the students so that they are engaged and motivated to learn.

How do you think teacher preparation programs should be training teachers to teach in your schools?

Ben Daley, chief academic officer of High Tech High, has interviewed hundreds of teachers over the years and recognizes that teachers lack the ability to apply the information they learned from their schooling. For the most part programs do not cover any information on project-based learning. They come to High Tech High lacking an understanding of how to use innovative teaching approaches that engage students in this methodology.

Educators also lack the ability to apply the methods and techniques they learned in their programs because they were not provided enough opportunities to apply information immediately after learning it. Programs tend to emphasize theoretical concepts but are lacking in practical applications of these concepts. Teacher candidates have told him that much of their course work was not relevant to them and they had to learn how to teach during their first year of teaching.

What does your organization do to prepare teachers to teach in your schools?

High Tech High is unique in that they created their own teacher licensure program. This organization hires individuals they believe fit their school model and train them while they are teaching. It is similar to on-the-job training programs, except that many of their teachers have an educational background in teaching and learning. Ben gave me an example of how they hired a PhD in biology who did not have teacher licensure, but this individual became a successful teacher at High Tech High after going through their program.

The program is designed in a way so that teachers can take course work once a week in the evenings and immediately apply this information in their classrooms. The applying of information learned in their evening courses occurs simultaneously with their teaching because they take the information learned and use it the next day in their classrooms. There is no lag time between theory and application. In many traditional teacher preparation programs, students learn theories and techniques but are not provided opportunities to apply the information until they do their student teaching, which usually occurs in the fourth or fifth year of their program. The High Tech High program requires two years of course work and culminates with a portfolio that highlights all the competencies required by the state of California to become a fully licensed teacher.

In addition, High Tech High has created a master's degree program in teacher leadership and another in school leadership. The teacher leadership program is for teachers who want to continue their professional development and learn cutting-edge theories and techniques that will help them become more effective teachers, and the school leadership degree is for individuals who desire to become administrators in schools. Both programs are two years in length, with course work occurring in the evenings. These programs emphasize a concept called "putting it to practice," which is similar to their teacher licensure program, in that these individuals immediately apply what they are learning as teachers and future administrators.

Each program has its own set of requirements. The teacher leadership program requires students to do an action research project where teachers identify a problem to solve in their classroom and, through the action research model, conduct research on the problem and work toward a resolution. The school leadership program requires individuals to do a leadership project, create a leadership philosophy statement, and create a school design plan. Individuals in this program are also required to spend a full year in a school working under a school administrator mentor (personal communication, May 31, 2011).

New Tech Network (NTN)

Local business leaders were concerned about creating a school to help students develop important skills that would allow them to succeed in college and the workplace, and after many discussions, the first New Tech School, called the Napa New Tech High School, began operation in 1996. The success of this first school led to a $6 million grant from the Bill and Melinda Gates Foundation, which allowed New Tech to launch fourteen more schools. Currently, the New Tech Network supports sixty-two schools in fourteen states (New Tech Network website, n.d.).

Their school model focuses on three primary ideas: the use of project-based learning; the use of smart technology; and creating a culture of trust, respect, and responsibility. PBL allows students to work together on relevant projects, which helps enhance their motivation to learn. All the classrooms are equipped with a one-to-one computer ratio for students. This allows students to rely less on teachers and to become researchers as they find necessary information to create and build their projects. Finally, New Tech schools foster an atmosphere of trust and respect by having students work together on projects and be responsible to their peers by completing individual tasks that are necessary to complete the group project.

Project-based learning is at the core of the learning process. Students have the freedom to do their research on their own computers, and the teachers act as guides in the learning process. Most projects require collaboration from all students as they work toward completing their group projects. Students at New Tech High schools learn important life skills like responsibility, communication, and teamwork.

How do you think teacher preparation programs should be training teachers to teach in your schools?

Tim Presiado, senior director of new school development at New Tech Network, believes that in order to prepare students for college and career, teachers need to be able to teach and assess both academic content and deeper learning skills, such as collaboration, critical thinking, communication, and creativity. Teacher preparation programs can support this effort by exposing their teachers to student-centered teaching models such as project-based learning. In order to support this shift in pedagogy and thinking, programs need to support teachers in their ability to analyze and map standards to authentic challenges and problems and help them develop assessment tools that focus the formative and summative assessment of student work on both academic content and skills for college and career readiness.

As educators make a shift toward student-centered, collaborative models, teachers need training in collaborative learning techniques. At New Tech High, the PBL process requires students to work in groups and be responsible for doing tasks that help the group complete the project. Since this learning environment is drastically different from a traditional learning environment, teachers often lack experience in supporting and facilitating groups of students throughout a project. Teacher preparation programs could support new teachers in their readiness to work in a PBL classroom by focusing on collaborative learning and the scaffolding that is needed to ensure that all students can be successful in a group learning environment.

What does your organization do to prepare teachers to teach in your schools?

New Tech High has an interesting approach to training teachers. They believe that in order to prepare teachers to use PBL, entire schools and districts need to be educated on how to use this process. School districts work with New Tech Network for up to a year before the opening of the school. In this planning year, stakeholders including district, school, community, and business leaders visit existing New Tech schools to see and experience the pervasive transformation in school culture and instructional pedagogy across a school campus.

They believe that the transformation in instruction and the development of college- and career-ready students is built upon a highly personalized process that empowers students and teachers. Much of New Tech's training and support is focused on building school cultures and creating systems on a school campus that will allow all teachers to develop and implement standards-based projects throughout the school year.

Tim mentioned there were approximately 196 tours and training sessions last year to help New Tech open eighteen new schools in the fall of

2011. Teachers and administrators experience a variety of training lead-ing up to the opening of a New Tech school, such as leadership training for NT principals, shadowing for teachers in existing NT schools, and a five-day training program in the summer that focuses on project-based learning, the deep integration of technology, and the development of school culture. A hallmark of all New Tech training is that the New Tech Network uses the PBL process in all of their events, to put teachers and administrators in the role of student. This allows the New Tech facilitators and coaches to model the PBL process, and it lets the participants experi-ence this pedagogical approach firsthand.

NTN training events provide teachers with an opportunity to develop standards-focused PBL units and to receive feedback from NTN coaches and active teachers from across the network. This support from other New Tech practitioners allows teachers to revise their project ideas and offer ideas on how to assess these projects. Ongoing support throughout the school year is critical to the sustained success and implementation of PBL.

NTN provides on-the-ground and remote coaching targeted at both teachers and leaders. One of the primary objectives for NTN is that schools have the ability to sustain their long-term development by train-ing and coaching their own staff in PBL practices. For this reason, New Tech Network certifies teachers, trainers, and schools to enable ongoing improvement, refinement, and sustainability (T. Presiado, personal com-munication, June 6, 2011).

Gateway to College National Network (GtCNN)

Gateway to College was started as a way to help high school dropouts reconnect with education and earn a high school diploma while also re-ceiving college credits for their work. It started in 2000 at Portland Com-munity College and now has a network of thirty colleges in sixteen states (Gateway to College website, n.d.). Like other successful school models, the Bill and Melinda Gates Foundation provided funding for them, recog-nizing that the model provides students with a chance to finish their high school education as well as receive college credits. This program is dif-ferent from the others in that they are housed at community colleges and focus on pulling dropout students back to school.

GtCNN created a second program called Project DEgree, which targets college students needing remedial work with goals of significantly increasing the number of students transitioning into college-level course work and then graduating from college. Project DEgree programs are currently housed at nine community colleges nationally.

Their design essentials were created for community colleges wishing to participate in these two programs. The principles include intentional collaboration, integrated leadership, innovative teaching and learning, and holistic student support. Their design essentials are designed for administrators and faculty working at these community colleges, with a strong emphasis on preparing faculty to design integrated project-based curriculums structured around a learning community and using innovative approaches to teaching and student support.

Faculty members learn to collaborate with one another and create assignments that are interconnected with other subject areas so that students can connect content from one course to another. Administrators must be involved in the process and understand how these programs can be integrated into the community college mission.

Teaching and learning principles emphasize a combination of academic and life skills. Participating colleges must also agree to provide students with holistic support that includes both intellectual and emotional help when necessary.

Like many of the other schools discussed in this chapter, integrated project-based design plays a significant role in their Principles of Teaching and Learning. Faculty members are provided with the research evidence that connects project-based learning to higher levels of engagement, and they learn how to use PBL in their classrooms. Workshops are required for faculty members involved in these programs, and there are a number of workshops that help them effectively implement this approach.

How do you think faculty should be trained to teach in your programs?

Stephen Rice, director of organizational learning for Gateway to College National Network, mentioned that college faculty are often hired for their content knowledge and often need further training with pedagogical skills, specifically in the constructivist approach to learning. Like many teacher preparation programs that focus their training on direct instruction, many college faculty use this approach as well.

The faculty training offered by GtCNN models active teaching methods, giving faculty new ideas for conveying their content and facilitating engaging learning experiences for students. Training sessions first and foremost focus on building community among faculty so that they can share ideas and learn innovative techniques from each other. The goal of GtCNN training is to build on faculty expertise.

Training on integrated PBL design provides faculty with an impetus to collaborate that wouldn't normally exist. At the outset, instructors may have a sense of fear of the unknown, but this changes over time. This fear typically gives way to excitement when they share the creative process with other talented colleagues.

What does your organization do to prepare faculty to teach in your schools?

GtCNN provides faculty with an in-depth training program that includes instruction on how to integrate PBL into their curriculums. While service learning is gaining momentum in the postsecondary environment, integrated assignments and authentic assessment is new to many faculty, and they benefit from support with implementing those strategies. GtCNN provides two levels of training support for faculty. They begin by offering a two- or three-day workshop that provides faculty with training on their Principles of Teaching and Learning.

Their key teaching and learning principles include interdisciplinary learning where students are connecting ideas from one class or subject area to another; problem solving and critical thinking where students are engaged in rigorous projects that allow them to analyze, synthesize, and evaluate what they are learning; collaborative learning where students learn to work together and develop a mutual level of respect and support for one another; being actively involved in projects that require students to collaborate and learn by making mistakes; knowledge construction where students learn to make meaning of the experiences they undergo while completing projects; and personal growth where students learn to overcome self-defeating attitudes and move closer to becoming self-directed learners.

The second level of training is called the Instructional Coaching Program and lasts twelve to eighteen months, consisting of six on-site instructional coaching sessions that include observation and reflections for three semesters. Coaches work closely with faculty, observing them while they are implementing the Principles of Teaching and Learning in their classrooms and offer suggestions on how to improve.

Faculty members create improvement plans that they implement in their classrooms. After coaches observe faculty members, a series of discussions occur between faculty members and coaches. Faculty members reflect on their teaching experiences and discussions with coaches and begin to better understand how to implement the Principles of Teaching and Learning, which include PBL (S. Rice, personal communication, May 31, 2011).

UPSHOT FROM THE INTERVIEWS

All the interviewed stakeholders from these organizations recognize that educators are not receiving the necessary training and education to work in these innovative programs. Teacher preparation programs are not informing teacher candidates about these new school models, nor are they teaching them how to implement experiential approaches like project-based learning. Through their own personal experiences, these programs have come to realize that they must retrain educators to fit their models because they lack understanding and experience with these new teaching approaches.

The teaching approaches promoted by these organizations are obviously quite different from direct instruction, which is used by many traditional mainstream schools. Teachers and schools that use these approaches find that students take more control of their own learning by choosing projects, activities, and field experiences that are relevant and meaningful to their own lives.

The theoretical underpinnings of these organizations rely heavily on Dewey's (1938) "pattern of inquiry." The pattern of inquiry consists of six steps; however, Dewey's theory is similar to the scientific method that consists of four basic steps (pp. 101–119). He explains that a relevant problem (step one) causes perplexity and desire to find an answer, which is then followed by creating a plan (step two), testing the plan against reality (step three), and reflecting on its worth (step four).

The planning and testing phases of this learning process are critical. Designing and building projects, engaging in activities, or doing field-based work require students to create a plan before they begin and then use the plan to test out their ideas. Trial and error is crucial to this learning process, and making mistakes is a natural part of it. Responding to instructor questions and reciting back information, which is a common teaching method in traditional education, allows students to talk, but learning becomes inspirational and exciting when students create plans and test their plans against reality to determine their worth.

In traditional education, students are often penalized for making mistakes, and their grades are often lowered when mistakes are made, but at the schools described in this chapter, mistakes are a natural part of the learning process and are embraced by the teachers.

Creating a website, building a learning portfolio, performing an experiment, creating a piece of artwork, building something off a blueprint, or doing an internship all require critical thinking and problem-solving skills. For Dewey, learning meant doing something with the subject matter aside from reciting and memorizing it. Like Dewey's philosophy, these teachers and schools focus their attention on students' interests and allow them to choose relevant meaningful experiences. Students who attend these schools or programs are given the freedom to determine some of their own learning activities and work at their own pace, and the teachers act as guides to the learning process.

These schools treat students as adults. They allow them to explore their passions and provide them with a certain amount of freedom to learn what is relevant and important to them. Students enrolled in these schools and programs learn much more than just academic content; they learn about themselves, and they learn how to become lifelong learners.

Since these schools and programs are highly student centered and allow students freedom to work at their own pace, they provide opportunities to practice life skills such as time management, problem solving, and responsibility. Students learn not only academic content, but they also learn life skills that are critical in helping them become productive members of society.

Teacher preparation programs need to change now. Teacher candidates need to be provided information about these types of school models and the pedagogical techniques they use.

Chapter Six

Final Thoughts

So, where does all this leave the education system? Change is never a fast process in education, especially when it comes to changing one's personal values and beliefs. It appears that the business world is much quicker to respond to change and is more open-minded about eliminating policies and procedures that do not produce intended results. The education system needs to do the same.

Change is occurring, however, whether educators want it to or not. Here is a summary of the key changes that will help move the education system forward in a positive direction. All these changes are intricately woven together, and at the heart of these changes, which was mentioned at the outset of this book, is one primary goal: motivating students to learn, which will help keep them from dropping out of school.

THE LEARNING PROCESS

The education system has to broaden its view of learning. If it does not, then students will continue to be bored with their education and continue to drop out of school and college. The education system must view learning as a more complex process that allows students to practice life skills as they apply information, and to test out ideas to determine their value. Content knowledge is important to learn, but the primary goal should not focus on memorizing this content for a standardized test. The goal should be to have students learn life skills like critical thinking, problem solving, collaboration, and responsibility while they are engaged with academic content.

The most important life skill I learned was tenacity. I did not learn this in school; rather I learned it through the experiences I encountered outside the classroom. I learned it through multiple trial-and-error attempts while engaged in direct experience with life. I learned it by solving problems I encountered that did not have one specific answer. I learned it by interacting with things and people in real-world settings.

The education system needs to allow students to learn through direct experience, which entails making mistakes. The classroom should be used as a place where students research and gather information, and then they must be allowed opportunities to apply this information in real-life settings. This process will motivate them to learn and will allow them to learn important life skills.

If multiple-choice tests are the only assessment tool used to measure students' intelligence against the rest of the world, then the education system in the United States will continue to lose ground. An education system that focuses on helping students develop life skills will gain ground because students will graduate from high school as self-directed learners, ready to tackle the problems and challenges they will face in life, regardless of whether they attend college or not.

NO CHILD LEFT BEHIND

No Child Left Behind legislation must be eliminated or revised. There are too many standards and benchmarks that teachers do not have enough time to cover during the school year. This creates a situation that echoes back to the learning process, where teachers lecture because it is the most efficient way to disburse large amounts of information in short amounts of time. The learning that results from this process is memorization of information, but this information will be useless if students forget it shortly after taking the tests.

Content standards need to be minimized so teachers can adequately cover them, and then students must be allowed to apply this content. If the National Core Standards were adopted by all states, it would minimize the number of standards and could be an avenue for students to learn life skills.

New assessment tools need to be created that will measure life skills like problem solving, collaboration, and responsibility. The Educational Testing

Service must employ new types of tests that focus on formative assessment so that life skills can be measured periodically over the school year.

TEACHING APPROACHES

The most effective way to begin changing the learning process is to use teaching approaches that engage students in their learning. I have used all the approaches mentioned in chapter 3 and know from experience that they motivate students to learn. When the learning process starts with a problem, rather than information to be memorized, students begin to think.

Students think about potential solutions and begin to formulate ideas on how to solve the problem. They research ideas, ask questions, seek out individuals who have information they need, and interact with the subject matter on a deeper level. They are motivated by a challenge to discover an answer. All these approaches begin the learning process with a problem that tends to spark interest and in turn inspires students to search for answers.

These teaching approaches can begin to change the education system. Students do not want to be passive learners. Students want to interact with the subject matter and use it in ways that are relevant to their own lives.

When educators use these approaches and allow some freedom for students to choose projects and activities that are relevant to them, students begin to learn how to be self-directed learners. They learn how to learn, which is the most important goal of education.

PERFORMANCE-BASED ASSESSMENTS

Students should be learning life skills in school, and in order to learn these skills they must be provided opportunities to practice them. The current assessment system focuses heavily on practicing one skill: memorization. This skill does not help them become self-directed learners. Managing time, being responsible to group members, solving challenging problems, and learning from mistakes will help them become self-directed learners.

Teaching approaches that allow students to interact with the subject matter and with their peers, coupled with assessments that focus on measuring life skills, will help them learn skills required of them once they graduate from school. Performance-based assessments must be integrated in education so that students have opportunities to practice skills and observe these skills improve over time.

The current education system is standardized where all students move through it at the same pace, covering the same material, and taking the same tests. This is not the way people learn. People learn at different speeds, and the education system needs to consider adopting assessments that allow for individuality. Performance assessments would allow students to learn at their own speeds.

Performance-based assessments would allow students to learn life skills at their own pace and see them improve over time. Students need to be allowed to practice life skills on an ongoing basis because it takes time to learn these skills; it does not happen overnight.

Performance is just that: performing a skill. Performance assessments fit perfectly with the teaching approaches mentioned in this book because students must be engaged with the subject matter and learn through direct experience in real-life settings.

The Educational Testing Service and policy makers must change their views on assessment and incorporate more formative assessments in the education system. One could argue that these assessments are more subjective, but summative assessments are also highly subjective. Evaluating student learning is always a challenging process; however, performance assessments would at least allow students to practice important life skills, regardless of how fast they learn them, and would allow them to be tested periodically during the school year to show improvement.

TEACHER PREPARATION

Teachers are not being educated on how to use new approaches that engage students in their learning. New school models continue to crop up all across the U.S., and educators do not know how to teach in these new schools. This situation forces school development organizations to retrain their teachers, which is not an efficient use of their time.

Education is changing and will continue to change, which means teacher preparation programs must make teacher candidates aware of new teaching approaches and how to implement them in these new schools.

Teacher candidates deserve to be educated about new innovative models and approaches so they can make informed decisions on where they would like to be employed.

Currently teacher preparation programs focus all their attention on how to teach in mainstream traditional schools, which is a disservice to those wishing to teach in innovative schools. Teacher candidates deserve to be fully educated on all approaches and models of schooling so they can pursue a career path that fits their own personal philosophy of education.

I will leave parents and educators with one final question: what do you want your children to learn from their education? If you want them to learn how to learn and how to become self-directed learners, then you must engage in conversations with your schools on how educators can teach life skills that will allow your children to tackle challenging problems they will face as adults when they enter the realities of life outside of school.

References

Amrein-Beardsley, A., Berliner, D. C., & Rideau, S. (2010). Cheating in the first, second, and third degree: Educators' responses to high-stakes testing. *Educational Policy Analysis Archives, 18*(14). Retrieved October 30, 2010, from http://epaa.asu.edu/ojs/article/view/714.

Astin, A., & Oseguera, L. (2002). *Degree attainment at American colleges and universities.* Los Angeles: University of California, Higher Education Research Institute.

Barkley, E., Cross, K. P., & Howell Major, C. (2004). *Collaborative learning techniques: A handbook for college faculty.* San Francisco: Jossey-Bass.

Barrows, H. S., & Tamblyn, R. H. (1980). *Problem based learning: An approach to medical education.* New York: Springer.

Batista Schlesinger, A. (2009). *The death of why: The decline of questioning and the future of democracy.* San Francisco: Berrett-Koehler Publishers.

Big Picture Learning website. (n.d.). Retrieved May 23, 2011, from http://www.bigpicture.org/schools.

Billing, S. H. (2000). Research on K–12 school-based service-learning: The evidence builds. *Phi Delta Kappan, 81*(9), 658–664.

Blackburn, R. T., Pellino, G. R., Boberg, A., & O'Connell, C. (1980). Are instruction improvement programs off target? *Current Issues in Higher Education, 2*(1), 32–48.

Blumenfeld, P., Soloway, E., Marx, R., Krajcik, J., Guzdial, M., & Palincsar, A. (1991). Motivating project-based learning: Sustaining the doing, supporting the learning. *Educational Psychologist, 26*(3/4), 369–398.

Bridgeland, J., DiIulio, J., & Morison, K. (2006). *The silent epidemic: Perspectives of high school dropouts.* Washington, DC: Civic Enterprises.

Brookfield, S. D. (2006). *The skillful teacher.* San Francisco: Wiley.

Brookfield, S., & Preskill, S. (2005). *Discussion as a way of teaching.* San Francisco: Jossey-Bass.

Brophy, J. (2008). Developing student's appreciation for what is taught in school. *Educational Psychologist, 43*(3), 132–142.

Bruffee, K. A. (1995). Sharing our toys: Cooperative learning versus collaborative learning. *Change,* January/February, 12–18.

Center on Education Policy. (2010). How many schools have not made adequate yearly progress under the No Child Left Behind Act? Retrieved October 30, 2010, from http://www.cepdc.org/index.cfm?fuseaction=document_ext.show DocumentByID&nodeID=1&DocumentID=303.

Christensen, C., Johnson, C., & Horn, M. (2010). *Disrupting class: How disruptive innovation will change the way people learn.* New York: McGraw-Hill.

College Board website. Advanced Placement history questions. Retrieved October 26, 2010, from http://www.collegeboard.com/student/testing/ap/history _ussamp.html?ushist.

Common Core State Standards for English Language Arts and Literacy in History/Social, Science, and Technical Subjects. (2010). Retrieved April 11, 2011, from http://www.corestandards.org.

Cress, C. M., Collier, P. J., & Reitenauer, V. L. (2005). *Learning through serving: A student guidebook for service-learning across the disciplines.* Sterling, VA: Stylus.

Delisle, R. (1997). *How to use problem-based learning in the classroom.* Alexandria, VA: Association for Supervision and Curriculum Development.

Dewey, J. (1938). *Logic: The theory of inquiry.* New York: Holt, Rinehart & Winston.

———. (1973). Pattern of inquiry. In J. J. McDermott (Ed.), *The philosophy of John Dewey* (pp. 223–239). Chicago: University of Chicago Press. (Reprinted from *Logic: The theory of inquiry,* pp. 101–119, by J. Dewey, 1938, Austin, TX: Holt, Rinehart & Winston.)

Duncan, A. (2010). *The quiet revolution.* U.S. Department of Education. Retrieved October, 27, 2010, from http://www.ed.gov/news/speeches/quiet -revolution-secretary-arne-duncans-remarks-national-press-club.

EdVisions home page. (2008). Retrieved December 17, 2008, from http://edvisions.com.

Expeditionary Learning. (2011). *Expeditionary Learning core practices.* New York: Author.

Expeditionary Learning website. (n.d.). *About us: History.* Retrieved May 24, 2011, from http://elschools.org/about-us/history.

———. (n.d.). *What we do.* Retrieved May 25, 2011, from http://elschools.org/ our-approach/what-we-do.

Eyler, J., & Giles, D. E. (1999). *Where's the learning in service-learning?* San Francisco: Jossey-Bass.

Gardner, H. (1991). *The unschooled mind: How children think and how schools should teach.* New York: Basic Books.

———. (2006). *Multiple intelligences: New horizons.* New York: Basic Books.

Gateway to College website. (n.d.). Retrieved June 8, 2011, from http://www.gatewaytocollege.org/home.asp.

Grant, M., & Branch, R. (2005). Project-based learning in a middle school: Tracing abilities through the artifacts of learning. *Journal of Research on Technology in Education, 38*(1), 65–98.

Greene, J. P., & Winters, M. A. (2006). The boys left behind: The gender graduation gap. *National Review*, April. Retrieved June 6, 2007, from http://www.nationalreview.com/comment/greene_winters200604190558.asp.

Gould, D., & Carson, S. (2008). Life skills development through sport: Current status and future directions. *International Review of Sport and Exercise Psychology, 1*(1), 58–78.

High Tech High. (n.d.). *Design principles.* Retrieved June 6, 2011, from http://www.hightechhigh.org/about/design-principles.php.

Hoover, S. (2006). Popular culture in the classroom: Using video clips to enhance survey classes. *History Teacher, 39*(4), 467–478.

Huba, M. E., & Freed, J. E. (2000). *Learner-centered assessment on college campuses: Shifting the focus from teaching to learning.* Needham Heights, MA: Allyn & Bacon.

Johnson, L. F., Smith, R. S., Smythe, J. T., & Varon, R. K. (2009). *Challenge-based learning: An approach for our time.* Retrieved March 5, 2011, from images.apple.com/education/docs/Apple-challenged-based-learning.pdf.

Kaye, C. B. (2004). *The complete guide to service learning.* Minneapolis, MN: Free Spirit Publishing.

Lawhorn, B. (2008). Extracurricular activities: The afterschool connection. *Occupational Outlook Quarterly, 52*(4), 16–21.

Levine, E. (2002). *One kid at a time: Big lessons from a small school.* New York: Teachers College Press.

Levitt, R., & Candiotti, S. (2011). Mother hopes others will opt out of standardized testing. CNN U.S. Retrieved March 25, 2011, from http://articles.cnn.com/2011-03-20/us/pennsylvania.school.testing_1_standardized-tests-schools-park-forest-elementary?_s=PM:US.

Levitz, R., Noel, L., & Richter, B. (1999). Strategic moves for retention success. *New Directions for Higher Education, 27*(4), 31–49.

Littky, D., & Grabelle, S. (2004). *The big picture: Education is everyone's business*. Alexandria, VA: Association for Supervision and Curriculum Development (ASCD).

Markham, T., Larmer, J., & Ravitz, J. (2003). *Project based learning handbook: A guide to standards-focused project based learning for middle and high school teachers*. Novato, CA: Buck Institute for Education.

Maxwell, N. L., Mergendoller, J. R., & Bellisimo, Y. (2005). Problem-based learning and high school economics: A comparative study of instructional methods. *Journal of Economic Education, 36*(4), 315–331.

Met Life Survey of the American Teacher. (2010). Retrieved March 29, 2011, from http://www.metlife.com/about/corporate-profile/citizenship/metlife-foundation/metlife-survey-of-the-american-teacher.html.

Middendorf, J., & Kalish, A. (1996). The change up in lectures. *The National Teaching and Learning Forum, 5*(2). Retrieved February 28, 2009, from http://www.ntlf.com/html/pi/9601/article1.htm.

Minnesota Department of Education. (2009). Minnesota academic standards in science, grades K–12. Retrieved April 11, 2011, from http://education.state.mn.us/mdeprod/groups/Standards/documents/Publication/013906.pdf.

Minnesota New Country School. (2007). *A study of the Minnesota New Country School: District #4007*. Retrieved April 23, 2008, http://www.newcountryschool.com/media/EDocs/Annual_Report_0607.pdf.

Muir, G. M., & van der Linden, G. J. (2009). Students teaching students: An experiential learning opportunity for large introductory psychology classes in collaboration with local elementary schools. *Teaching of Psychology, 36*(3), 169–173.

National Center for Public Policy and Higher Education. (2006). *Measuring up 2006: The national report card on higher education*, p. 7. Retrieved May 12, 2008, from http://www.highereducation.org/reports/mup_06/MUP-06.pdf.

Newbrey, M. G., & Baltezore, J. M. (2006). Poster presentations: Conceptualizing, constructing, and critiquing. *American Biology Teacher, 68*(9), 550–554.

Newell, R. (2003). *Passion for learning: How project-based learning meets the needs of 21st-century students*. Lanham, MD: Scarecrow Press.

———. (2005). Student ownership: Teacher ownership. In D. Thomas, W. Enloe, & R. Newell (Eds.), *The coolest school in America: How small learning communities are changing everything* (pp. 19–27). Lanham, MD: Rowman & Littlefield.

Newell, R., & Van Ryzin, M. (2007). Growing hope as a determinant of school effectiveness. *Phi Delta Kappan, 88*(6), 465–471.

———. (2009). *Assessing what really matters in schools: Creating hope for the future*. Lanham, MD: Rowman & Littlefield.

New Media Consortium. *Challenge-based learning: An approach for our time.* Retrieved June 26, 2011, from www.nmc.org/pdf/Challenge-Based-Learning.pdf.

New Tech Network website. (n.d.). Retrieved June 8, 2011, from http://www.newtechnetwork.org/node/62.

Partnership for 21st Century Skills website. Retrieved June 26, 2011, from www.p21.org.

Popham, W. J. (2008). *Transformative assessment.* Alexandria, VA: Association for Supervision and Curriculum Development.

Project learning links school with "after school." (2011). *American Teacher 95*(6), 4.

Ramsey, J., & Sorel, E. (2007). Problem based learning: An adult-education-oriented training approach for SH&E practitioners. *Professional Safety: American Society of Safety Engineers* (September), 41–46.

Ravitch, D. (2010). *The death and life of the great American school system: How testing and choice are undermining education.* New York: Basic Books.

Rubenstein, G. (2007). Confronting the crisis in teacher training. Edutopia website. Retrieved May 9, 2011, from: http://www.edutopia.org/schools-of-education.

Sax, L. J., Keup, J. R., Gilmartin, S. K., Stolzenberg, E. B., & Harper, C. (2002). *Findings from the 2000 administration of "Your First College Year": National aggregates.* Los Angeles: University of California, Higher Education Research Institute.

Secretary's Commission on Achieving Necessary Skills, U.S. Department of Labor. (2001). Learning a living: A blueprint for high performance. A SCANS report for America: 2000 executive summary principles and recommendations. In *The Jossey-Bass Reader on School Reform.* San Francisco: Jossey-Bass.

Soslau, E., & Yost, D. (2007). Urban service-learning: An authentic teaching strategy to deliver a standards-driven curriculum. *Journal of Experiential Education, 30*(1), 36–53.

Stiggins, R. J., Arter, J. A., Chappuis, J., & Chappuis, S. (2006). *Classroom assessment for student learning.* Princeton, NJ: Educational Testing Services.

Teaching Performance Assessment. (n.d.). Retrieved April 30, 2011, from http://ed.fullerton.edu/SecEd/tpa/index.htm.

Technology Applications Center for Educator Development. Oral rubric: Instructions. Retrieved October 26, 2010, from http://www.tcet.unt.edu/START/instructgeneral/oral.htm.

Temes, Peter. (2003). *Against school reform (and in praise of great teaching): Getting beyond endless testing, regimentation, and reform in our schools.* Lanham, MD: Ivan R. Dee.

Thomas, D., Enloe, W., & Newell, R. (2005). *The coolest school in America: How small learning communities are changing everything.* Lanham, MD: Scarecrow Education.

U.S. Department of Education. (2006). *Charter high schools: Closing the achievement gap.* Retrieved April 11, 2011, from http://www2.ed.gov/admins/comm/choice/charterhs/report_pg18.html#mncs.

U.S. Department of Labor. SCANS Report. Retrieved November 5, 2010, from http://wdr.doleta.gov/SCANS.

Vansteenkiste, M., Lens, W., & Deci, E. (2006). Intrinsic versus extrinsic goal contents in self-determination theory: Another look at the quality of academic motivation. *Educational Psychologist, 41*, 19–31.

Wagner, T. (2008). *The global achievement gap.* New York: Basic Books.

What work requires of schools: A SCANS report for America 2000. Retrieved November 5, 2010, from http://wdr.doleta.gov/SCANS/whatwork.

Wolk, R.A. (2001). Bored of education. *Teacher Magazine, 13*(3), 3.

Wurdinger, S. D., & Carlson, J. A. (2009). *Teaching for experiential learning: Five approaches that work.* Lanham, MD: Rowman & Littlefield.

Wurdinger, S. D., & Enloe, W. (2011). Cultivating life skills at a project-based charter school. *Improving Schools, 14*(1), 84–96.

Wurdinger, S., Haar, J., Hugg, B., & Bezon, J. (2007). A qualitative study using project-based learning in a mainstream middle school. *Improving Schools, 10*(2), 150–161.

Wurdinger, S. D., & Rudolph, J. L. (2009). A different type of success: Teaching important life skills through project-based learning. *Improving Schools, 12*(2), 117–131.

Yazzie-Mintz, E. (2006). *Voices of students on engagement: A report on the 2006 High School Survey of Student Engagement.* Bloomington, IN: Author.